To Florence Fryar
My much loved Nannie

"She seeketh wool, and flax, and
worketh willingly with her hands...
She layeth her hands to the
spindle, and her hands hold the distaff.
She stretcheth out her hand to
the poor; yea, she reacheth forth her
hands to the needy.
She is not afraid of the snow
for her household: for all her household
is clothed with embroidery."

Proverbs 31 vv 13, 19-22

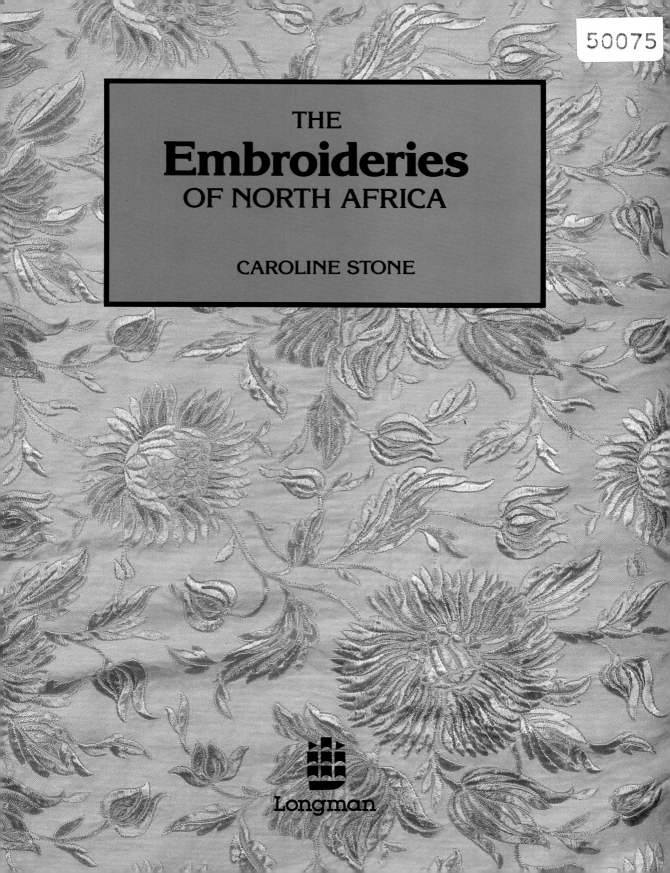

THE
Embroideries
OF NORTH AFRICA

CAROLINE STONE

Longman

Longman Group Limited,
Longman House,
Burnt Mill,
Harlow, Essex,
CM20 2JE

Associated companies and branches throughout
the world

First published 1985

ISBN 0 582 78371 2

British Library Cataloguing in Publication Data

Stone, Caroline
    Embroideries of North Africa.
    1. Embroidery — Africa, North
    I. Title
    746.44′0961   NK9287.6

ISBN 0-582-78371-2

Set in Linotron 202 Korinna 11/13 pt

Printed in Great Britain
by William Clowes Ltd, Beccles & London

endpaper: Detail from 18th-century Algerian
          embroidery

title page: Detail from Tétouan Shawl

CONTENTS

Paris

Venice
Genoa
Ravenna
Pisa
Assisi
Rome

ADRIAT

CORSICA

SARDINIA

Lisbon
Toledo

BALEARIC IS

MEDITERR

Palermo
SICILY

San Lucar
Ronda
Cadiz
Granada
Algiers
Constantine
Bône
Tunis
Béja
Bou Kornein
Cap Bon
MALTA

Tangiers
Ceuta
Tétouan
Chechouan
Oran
Tlemcen
Kairouan
Sfax

Rabat
Salé
Fez
Casablanca
Meknès
Gafsa
Volubilis
Nefta
Gabès
Azemmour
Médinine
MOROCCO
ALGERIA
Chenini
Tripoli
TUNISIA

BouReg-Reg

Oum er-Riba

Marrakesh

to: Walata
Shingit

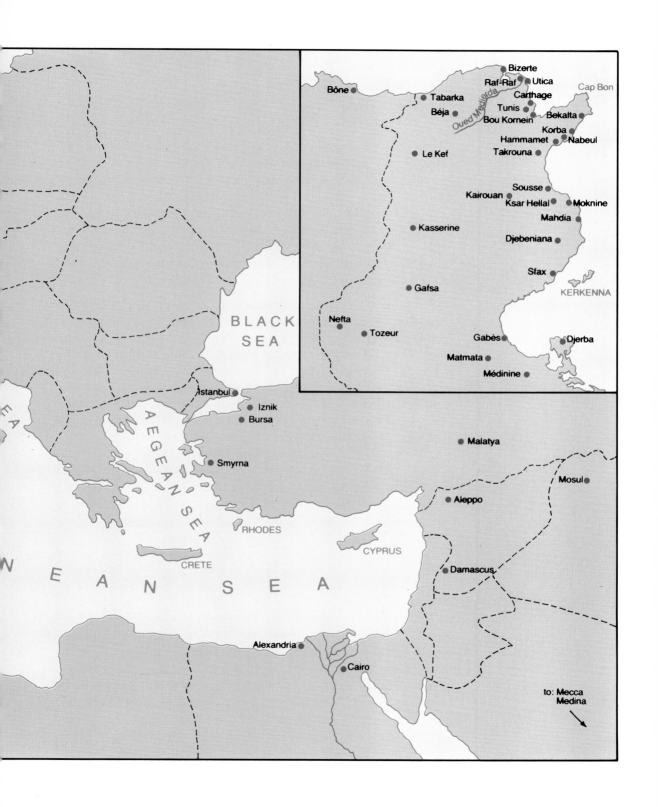

INTRODUCTION

As I collected material for this book, I quickly came to understand what a great deal there was to know and to find out, and also to realize that I was not going to have time to examine everything in the depth that it deserved. There are, therefore, blanks, most particularly as regards Algeria, which I have not unfortunately had the opportunity to visit. I am very aware of these shortcomings and would consequently be immensely grateful to any kind reader who felt like picking up his or her pen and correcting my mistakes or telling me some of the many things I do not know.

The book was originally intended to cover all North Africa excluding Libya, which has almost no indigenous embroidery. In fact, I found it necessary for practical reasons to limit myself both geographically and technically. I have therefore tried to cover the main urban styles of Morocco (it proved impossible to find out enough about the rural ones to make it worthwhile including them) and the urban and village needlework of Tunisia. In the latter case it has been necessary to say something about costume since, unlike Morocco, most embroidery is done on pieces of clothing.

The section on Algeria is, as I have already explained, minimal; this is not a reflection on the quality or quantity of Algerian work, but on my ignorance and the lack of examples in European collections. It seemed better to say something, even a very little, to indicate that there is in fact a continuity all along the North African coast, than to leave it out altogether.

In the same spirit, I have just touched on Turkish embroideries, since they are found all over North Africa and it is not possible to appreciate their influence without having an idea of what they are like.

There are a number of needlework techniques which I have referred to only briefly: embroidery on leather, gold embroidery, braids, trimmings and passementerie. This is partly because my main interest is in women's domestic embroideries. These tend to be silk or wool, done at home for the use of the household or commissioned by a known client. The other types are quite largely produced by men, almost always for sale on the open market and seem to me more standardized and less personal. Also, they have been well-studied from various points of view, including those of economics and guild organization (see bibliography). I have, therefore said only a minimum about them — just enough to remind readers that they exist.

Although North Africa is a weaving rather than embroidery culture, I have firmly resisted straying into the field of kelims, mergoum and so on.

This book has three main sources.

First of all, there are the numerous superb articles, mostly by French scholars, without which it could not have been written at all. I have referred to these sources in the text by the name of the author and, since the articles are usually quite short and with self-evident titles, the reader should be able to find them easily in the bibliography. For example, if I say in the section on Rabat: "Mme Brunot-David says...", her actual work can be ascertained by looking up Brunot-David, C. in the bibliography under Morocco, where *Les Broderies de Rabat* and the appropriate references are given. This has two advantages: it saves footnotes and makes it quite clear to whom I owe specific pieces of information.

The second source is more diffuse.

I am greatly indebted to numerous embroiderers and embroideresses, to owners of antique and junk shops, to assistants in the official centres of Artisanat and in small boutiques in the back-streets of the medinas of many cities, to market women from Tozeur to the Rif, who patiently answered my questions or allowed me to stand around watching them at work or let me examine their wares for hours at a time. Without them – and without Paul Lunde who tirelessly interpreted and even more tirelessly stood and waited – this book would have been impossible.

Thirdly, there are the museums, in North Africa itself – these are mentioned repeatedly in the text – and in France and England. The best collection in Europe is probably that of the Musée National des Arts Africains et Océaniens in Paris, where a wide range of Tunisian, Algerian and Moroccan embroideries are attractively displayed in a context of carpets, furniture and artifacts. There is also a considerable reserve collection.

In England there appears to be very little Tunisian embroidery, but the Whitworth Museum in Manchester, where, I would like to say, the staff were more than kind and patient with me, have a representative collection of Moroccan embroideries and one or two Algerian pieces. Roughly the same is true of the Fitzwilliam Museum, Cambridge. The Victoria and Albert Museum, London, should have a good number of North African embroideries, including some fine Algerian pieces but I have never been privileged to see them.

Some of the styles of traditional embroidery in North Africa are dead or dying. I rather hoped that by recording them in a book it might encourage interest in them and even, conceivably, help persuade the local Artisanats (government bodies for promoting arts and crafts) to teach their embroideresses to copy them. Even if initially they only reached the tourist market, it would at least ensure that the techniques and patterns were preserved and would mean that they could one day be readopted by the locals themselves and so become "alive" again.

Secondly, by giving outlines of motifs and some information on colours and stitches, I thought that embroideresses in Europe, or elsewhere, might like to add some new, pretty and not very demanding designs to their repertoire. I can think of nothing nicer than that this book should stimulate someone to pick up a strip of cloth and some thread and record – say – a wedding, a bunch of flowers or a shoal of fish in one of the various styles described, for example in the rough, naive, and in needlework terms "illiterate", but very effective, manner of Gabès and the Tunisian south.

Thirdly, this book may be of use to textile collectors and antique dealers who want to identify the odd pieces of North African embroidery that reach this country. They are, for obvious historical reasons, much more commonly offered for sale in France.

Lastly, I have tried to give the embroideries a slight historical and sociological context and thus the book may serve those who are interested in Tunisia and Morocco in a general way. North Africa has had numerous different cultural influences over the millennia, each of which has left some trace, and in considering the craft of any town or village it is relevant to have an idea of the history that lies behind it.

The reason then I have attempted this, admittedly sketchy, framework is that since nothing exists in a vacuum, it is more interesting to take a shred of embroidered cloth and to consider the criss-crossings of the Mediterranean and the slave-routes up through the Sahara and the indigenous tradition which brought it into being, than to see it exclusively in terms of x colours and y threads to the inch.

Again, by quoting poems and so on, I have tried to give an idea, even if only a minimal one, of what the embroideries meant to the women who made them and to those who wore them. They were decoration, of course, but they were more than that and had a weight and a meaning that we in the West, with mass-produced clothes and furnishings, have not only largely lost, but also, all too often, have forgotten ever existed.

It seems to me for reflective people – and there are many – it is stimulating to visit a country in the awareness that everything, even the most banal straw basket woven with a pattern of camels and sold at the airport, has a significance. It means something in terms of the culture – even if it only indicates the decadence of a tradition. Once this has been realized, everything becomes interesting, including things which are in themselves boring and ugly, because they are all pieces of the jigsaw. A new world, a new network of symbols, references, ideals, customs, concerns, beliefs, superstitions, begins to unfold. Inevitably, they are contrasted with the home equivalents. If nothing is known, the comparison may well be unfavourable to the less familiar country. But once it is realized that the porter in the hotel has tied a fish-tail to your suitcase, not because he is mad or has ideas which are hopelessly insanitary, but because he likes you and feels this will help protect your property from loss or theft, inevitably your attitude changes. Perhaps you will keep your fingers crossed or touch wood for him when he tries to get a visa to visit his son in Canada or when he goes to the dentist! In any case, it is likely that curiosity will have been aroused in setting in train the exciting process of discovering another culture and rediscovering one's own beginnings, in a personal and unacademic way.

This for me (leaving aside the sun and not having to do the washing up) is one of the great pleasures of travelling and I would be delighted if my book caused one or two people to look harder at the extraordinarily rich and mixed culture of North Africa, one of the rare and lucky areas of the world which seems to have been able both to conserve and to advance. The palaeolithic symbol of the hand; draped dresses which could usefully be compared with those of classical art; an archaic form of the Arabic language; fashions of Andalusian Spain and the Turkish court at Constantinople happily coexist with the most modern technology: subjects not for one book, but for a dozen.

Transliteration

I realize perfectly well that my transliteration of Arabic will either infuriate Arabists or cause them to sink their heads into their hands. It is not, however, as irrational as it looks. I have used the French conventions for transliterating North African dialect words and expressions for two reasons. Firstly, if the words are pronounced as if they were French, the speaker has a good chance of having them understood in North Africa, whereas the Classical equivalents will not be, since ordinary people in these countries do not speak Classical Arabic. Secondly, this is the way the words are spelt in the literature on the subject which is almost entirely French, and it seemed unfair to expect readers to battle with two different conventions of transliteration on top of a lot of completely unfamiliar words. I have, incidentally, spelt place names as they are spelt in the maps and on the road signs of the country in question.

It will be noticed that some words are spelt differently in the different sections. This again is an effort to conform to local practice and the glossary at the end of the book should serve to co-ordinate them.

For those with particular linguistic interests, *Les Costumes Traditionels Feminins de Tunisie* gives a very full glossary of Tunisian words for costume and textiles, including embroideries.

Embroidery in Islam

The whole question of embroidery in Islam is extremely complicated and much debated, and it is linked to the earlier question of the techniques in use in the Coptic, late-Classical and Byzantine world. This is not really the place to go into it in any detail, but those interested should consult the fifth volume of the second edition of the *Encyclopaedia of Islam* under the heading of *libas* – clothing – both for information and bibliography, and also the work of R.B. Sergeant (see bibliography).

A certain amount is known about the textiles, including embroideries, originating from the official factories – *tiraz* – which produced cloth and clothing intended for the ruler, either to use personally, or to give as marks of favour. These materials and robes of honour were generally worked with calligraphic inscriptions, either woven or embroidered. *Tiraz* existed in a number of cities, in North Africa principally at Kairouan, and examples of these very splendid materials have survived, often in church treasuries, and can sometimes be identified in paintings of the Middle Ages and Renaissance, after which the *tiraz* system essentially broke down. A particularly famous piece is the imperial mantle at Vienna, one of the most splendid of all mediaeval embroideries, made in the *tiraz* at Palermo in Sicily (see section on Mahdia for description) in 1134.

Tiraz, however, was very much the official textile industry. We know little about local or folk traditions, especially in North Africa where there is an extraordinary lack of both material and written sources between the coming of Islam and the 16th century. While I have tried to show the most probable influences on the different types of embroidery, the actual examples rarely, if ever, go back before the 18th century and more commonly belong to the 19th or 20th centuries.

The cloth of Egypt is like the white of an egg,
But the cloth of Yemen is like the flowers of spring.

Proverb.

*   *   *

Another hope I have, however, is that this book will stimulate the recording of embroidery patterns in other places, especially on the edges of the Islamic world such as Yemen, where it is likely that the older styles have survived, and where it might be possible to begin to reconstruct Islamic embroidery from its origins.

Patterns: natural and the stylized world

Besides the Koran itself and the Life of the Prophet, a very major source for Islamic law are the Traditions — stories concerning Muhammad and his deeds, collected after his death from those who knew him and lovingly handed down from generation to generation. One of the most important collections is that of al-Bukhari, which includes many accounts and anecdotes of the everyday life of the Prophet's household. The following tradition — or *hadith* — is one of many which explains why the human figure is not generally found in North African, or indeed in any Islamic, embroideries:

> "According to Ayesha (the Prophet's favourite wife), the Messenger of God came back one day from an expedition. 'As', she said, 'I had draped one of the corners of my room with a hanging of cloth that I possessed, ornamented with human figures, the Messenger of God saw it on entering and pulled it down, saying: "On the Day of Resurrection, the worst punishment will be inflicted on those who imitate the beings created by God." 'Then', said Ayesha, 'we made one or two cushions out of this material.' "

Bukhari (XCI/1)

There are numerous similar traditions. In one, Muhammad explains that the sight of the hanging distracted him from his prayers. XCII adds significantly that exception was made for "flower patterns on cloth." LXXXV (1 and 2) speak of the existence of the evil eye and the illicitness of tattooing. Yet others set forth the objections to Muslim men (but not women) wearing silk and gold; and the ideal mode of dress is given in some detail, largely based on the personal practice of Muhammad himself.

As in all cultures, religious prohibitions were more or less strictly observed depending on the temper of the times and local practice. North African women, especially in the South, are only now giving up tattooing, which was long considered erotic, as well as having all kinds of other significance, apparently more under the influence of the West than because of the attitude of Islam. On the other hand, the ban on representing the human figure clearly went deep and was very generally respected.

It was perhaps this attitude which led to the extreme stylization of such living things, including plants, that are represented. It is very obvious that no Tunisian, Algerian or Moroccan woman ever picked a flower and tried to embroider what she saw — although there are flowers everywhere. But this is not necessarily the result of Islam. It is a curious fact that peasants in constant contact with nature tend to stylize it and a taste for naturalism is usually the prerogative of the town-dweller. English and French "court" embroideries from the Middle Ages to the 19th century, Chinese court robes, the finest Turkish towels are all utterly urban and all attempt to portray recognizable, although usually conventional, flowers, fruit, butterflies and so on. The rural equivalents have typically reduced the original subjects to a barely decipherable hieroglyphic. The real world is not in itself interesting. If a rose is the symbol of love, there is no need for it to be realistic, assuming a series of, for example, nine cross-stitches arranged in a particular way will serve to convey the message.

Pauline Johnstone makes yet another point very clearly in her book on Greek embroidery:

> "Greek woman never appears to have turned to her surroundings for inspiration. She copied patterns used by her mother and her grandmother, and these in their turn were clearly taken from earlier embroidery, or textile, or pottery design. It is true that in many villages the patterns were given homely names (e.g. the walnut, the hen, etc.) but this appears to be because a certain pattern already known to them reminded women of these things…"
>
> *Greek Island Embroidery,* p.11

The same process may well have occurred to some extent with North African motifs.

Arab and Berber; city and country

In both Tunisia and Morocco, there is a considerable difference even today between the cities, especially those along the coast which have been urbanized for some 2500 years, and the countryside, the mountains and the fringe of the Sahara. In a rough and ready way, it can be said that the indigenous textile art of North Africa is weaving, and it is one at which the women of many areas, both Arab and Berber, excelled. Embroidery seems to have been a much more recent introduction and, by and large, an urban skill associated with the settlers from Andalusia, with the Turkish beys and their Circassian and Balkan harems, and with the general Mediterranean culture which inevitably influenced the cities on the sea.

I will now try to disentangle some of these strands.

"Power to our Lord" — a detail of a calligraphic inscription from 14th-century Granada. This style of writing, called thuluth, is traditionally considered to have been introduced, like so many other elegancies, into North Africa from Andalusia. It came to rival the much squarer local script based on Kufic and is still much used in gold embroidery. Here, in the original, the background is dark.

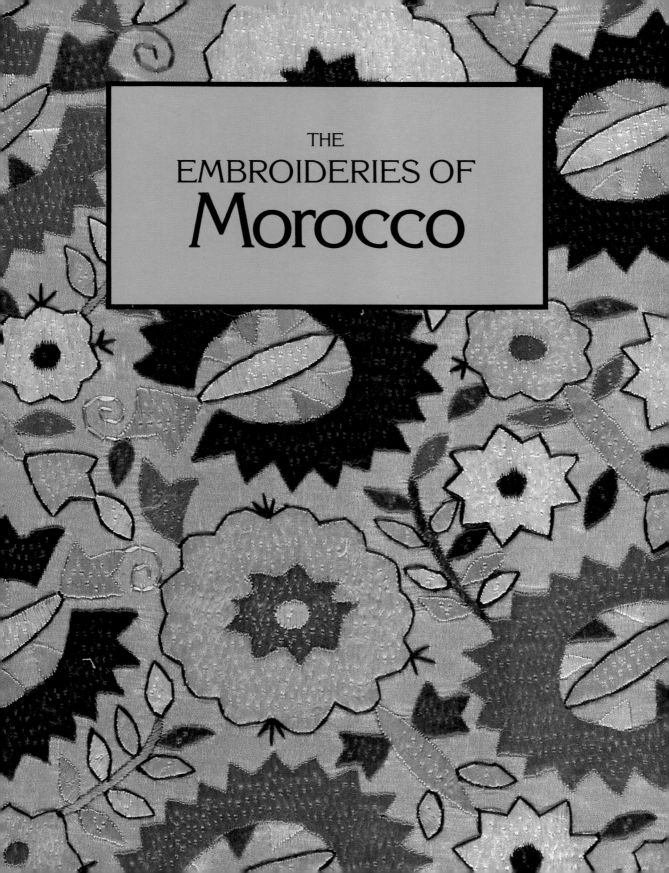

THE
EMBROIDERIES OF
Morocco

"In order to make the secret influence of the stars upon the world clear to the minds of men, the Chinese have devised a tangible symbol – the wooden loom on which they weave brocade. As the craftsman with his loom and spools of silk moves his shuttle back and forth across the warp, the design is born beneath his fingers. A throw of the shuttle and the wing of a bird takes shape, another and its head, a third and its legs are formed, and so on, until the workman's concept is complete. From this combination of the weaver's movements and the threads of the loom, the Chinese have made a symbol of the heavenly bodies and their effects upon the earth. One movement of a planet forms the bird, another its egg, a third the chick; in a word, all nature, movable and inert, living and dead, everything that joins and separates, that is united and sundered, that waxes and wanes, men and minerals, plants and animals, all these things here on earth, they say, result from the revolutions of the stars, just as the brocade results from the movements of the weaver at his loom."

Masudi, *The Meadows of Gold*, vol.IV, ch.LXIII, pp.53-4

Morocco, because of its heavily Berber population, is a weaving rather than an embroidering culture; nevertheless there are islands of embroidery and this embroidery is of two types. There is the silk or, now, cotton embroidery generally on cotton or linen, done by women, each of the embroidering cities having a completely different style, and there is the gold embroidery, essentially common to all of urban North Africa. As we are concerned with the former, we have arranged the description city by city and have tried to show how the history of each place – and their histories, although always turbulent, vary greatly – appears even in the simplest household objects, such as a mattress cover or a length of embroidered cloth.

AZEMMOUR

Azemmour is a small town on the coast below Casablanca and it stands at the mouth of the river Oum er-Rbia – "Mother of the Springtime". Little is known about its remote past, but from the 15th century it had intermittent though close trade links with Portugal, which in fact held it from 1514 to 1541. Among the goods bought by the Portuguese were *haiks* and *jellabas* – lengths of cloth and robes – and the Arab writers speak of clothes, though not embroideries, being exported from it at an early date. The town is famous for its pomegranates, its henna and its olive trees.

The embroidery

The embroideries of Azemmour are very distinctive. All the pieces consist of bands of rather heavy white cloth between 10 and 40 cm wide and up to 2.50 m long, embroidered in soft crimson or very deep blue silk. The pieces were presumably used to decorate mattress covers, the bottoms of curtains, and cushions. The stitches used are various forms of darning stitch, or sometimes chevron stitch and the occasional cross-stitch. It is typical of Azemmour embroidery that the ground is completely covered and that the design is made by the parts left white. The stitches themselves (as in area (b) of the Chéchaouen pieces, see page 20) are arranged into patterns, squares or a kind of Greek Key, and each little area is called a house or *bait*.

The older Azemmour embroideries are extremely rare and have very interesting designs. Unfortunately, I have not succeeded in seeing any of the earliest examples myself and am therefore relying on the illustrations given by P. Ricard and J. Jouin.

The Azemmour embroideries demonstrate beautifully what was said earlier about the exchange of motifs in the Mediterranean area. For some reason, hard to imagine without having a detailed knowledge of the history of the city, Azemmour retained a tradition of Renaissance Italian and Spanish patterns in its embroideries; and very close parallels can be found with the brown work from Toledo or the blue and black work from Assisi. Certainly, refugees from Spain arrived as a result of the fall of Granada in 1492 and the expulsion of the "Moors" by Philip III in 1610, but it is not clear why their influence and these particularly sophisticated motifs should have persisted in one small village rather than elsewhere on the coast.

The diffusion of such motifs is not in itself surprising, for, from the early 16th century, printed collections of embroidery patterns became very popular and spread all over Europe — although it is still hard to imagine one getting to Azemmour. The earliest seems to be *La Tagliente* of 1528, but there were numerous others and some, for example the *Livre de Lingerie* by Dominique de Sera, published in 1584, has designs almost indistinguishable from those of Azemmour, which, the author says in his preface, were collected in Spain.

Four of the most popular Azemmour patterns were:

1   The very favourite Christian (and of course before that Classical) motif of the vase flanked by doves, one of which may perch on the rim to slake its thirst, as in the famous Ravenna mosaic. Sometimes it is not the doves, in a Christian context symbolizing purity and reminiscent of the Holy Ghost, but the incorruptible peacock which comes to drink at the mystic vase of faith or immortality. It is a subject common in all the arts throughout the Mediterranean to the Greek Islands and even Turkey. Incidentally, St Augustine, himself a North African, is said to have tested the legend of the peacock's incorruptibility by taking a piece of the meat home from a feast to check. The Azemmour version of the vase and birds is often bordered by very stylized flowers or interspersed with cypresses or "trees of life", so formal as to suggest the Jewish *menorah* or seven-branched candlestick.

Azemmour: peacocks and vase.

2   Another motif which appears is the stylized woman with the full skirts. She set out, accompanied by a young lord or falconer, on the laces of Renaissance Venice to become one of the most popular patterns all over the Mediterranean, in embroidery, on cloth, on pots, on dower chests, appearing even as far north as

Russia, Norway and Sweden, and still surviving today, for example, in knitting. Mme Jouin in her article on Azemmour says: "I was much surprised to find a line of these male and female dancers in the costume of Henri II on an old Chichaouen [South Moroccan] carpet on view in the museum of Marrakesh." The same figure is to be found on some of the oldest embroideries from Rabat.

Of course, it should not be forgotten that this stylized figure of a woman, especially when, as at Rabat, the arms are raised, goes back far beyond the Renaissance to portrayals of such goddesses as Tanit — but this, and also the older significance of the doves will be discussed in the section on Tunisia.

3   Yet another theme is that of the chimaeras, or creatures like small dragons, either affronted or following each other, interspersed again with floral motifs or trees. These may be so stylized as to have become elaborate foliated scrolls.

Azemmour: monster and tree of life.

4   The pieces from Azemmour judged to be more recent (and the dating is very vague) have strange curvilinear patterns which seem to be decadent attempts at reproducing chimaeras, dragons, or possibly in some cases sirens — another motif which for millennia has haunted the Mediterranean. The human torso with two fish tails curving up on either side appears carved on an Etruscan tomb and also in Classical art, and reappears as a favourite decoration in the grotesques of the Renaissance. It was probably again via Italy that it spread to the

Greek Islands, and in particular Crete, but the creature was already strongly rooted in Mediterranean legend. Called Scylla or Gorgona, she was said to be the sister of Alexander the Great, who had cursed her and put a spell on her so that she would become half a fish and live in the sea for ever. Therefore, she asked each ship that passed: "Does King Alexander live?" for if he were dead no-one could ever lift the spell. If the correct reply came back: "He lives and reigns", she calmed the waves and let the ship go forward, but otherwise she would seize the bowsprit and drag it down into her kingdom below the sea.

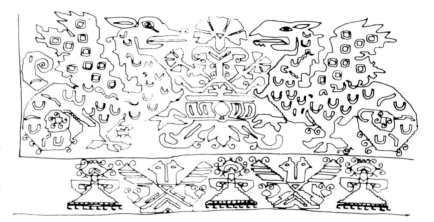

Azemmour motif: affronted griffins separated by a vase of flowers, with, below, alternating women and double-headed birds.

Unfortunately, with the later Azemmour embroideries, the white unworked ground which makes the pattern tends either to have become stained, or else blurred as the soft silk becomes fuzzy and spreads, thus making it almost impossible to photograph effectively.

As far as I could ascertain in Morocco, no-one has worked Azemmour embroidery for some fifty years.

CHÉCHAOUEN

Chéchaouen is an attractive small town in the mountains between Tétouan and Fez. It was founded in 1471 by Moulay Ali Ibn Rashid as a point from which to attack the Portuguese at Ceuta. Its fairly chequered history has included a number of contacts of one kind and another with the Iberian Peninsula. It may well be that, like Tétouan, refugees settled there after the fall of Granada in 1492 – certainly one of its quarters is still known as Rif al-Andalus.

The embroidery

One of the most beautiful and elaborate styles of Moroccan embroidery is said to come from Chéchaouen, although curiously there is no trace of its being made there today. Indeed, this was already the case in 1930 when Mme Jouin visited the town "and I was able to establish that the embroidery called Chéchaouen was completely unknown there. On the other hand it was known at Tétouan, where several families possessed examples and where there are still women, embroideresses working for wages, who are capable of doing it".

The classic embroideries of Chéchaouen are dated to the late 18th and early 19th centuries, and are very rare. Most of the existing pieces are fragments and it is often hard to know their original use. One thing appears certain: they were all furnishings – hangings, cushions and strips which are conventionally considered to be covers for chests, perhaps dower chests? The hangings are called 'arid and are said to have been hung from the carved or painted wall shelves or surrounds to the bed niches, which are such a feature of North African interiors, on feast days.

The lay-out of the basic Chéchaouen design is a curious one:

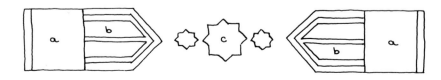

Chéchaouen Figure 1.

The design may be repeated again so that the two elements lie side by side, or at the top and bottom of the hanging, which might measure roughly 2 m × 2 m.

Mosaic square from Chéchaouen, late 18th or early 19th century

The background material is a strong white or natural linen with a clearly marked weave; later pieces may be worked on cotton, but in all cases the embroidery thread is silk.

The design has three main elements:

(a) Panels, more or less square – usually around 35 cm × 40 cm – known in French as "mosaics" and worked in some form of darning stitch. The best ones look like tapestry, the silk entirely covering the ground, and could be copied to very good effect in petit-point or cross-stitch, or to make a small rug. They have beautifully rich soft colours and the design is essentially geometric with very stylized floral elements. The two squares are typically not identical but complementary – one with a pattern based on a star, for example, and one on a roundel – and they use the same colour range. It has been pointed out that this effect has similarities to some of the cushions from Daghestan in the Caucasus. Perhaps even more significant are the relationships with Hispano-Mauresque embroideries, in particular the superb 15th-century embroidery of the Countess Ghisla, discussed most fascinatingly by Mme Jouin and Mme Guérard.

The ground of the mosaic panels tends to be yellow and the colours often recall those of Moroccan kelims. Typical combinations are: brick red/two tones of rather sombre blue/pale yellow/cream/a light, but not bright, green, with touches of other colours, and black or dark brown used to outline the elements of the pattern; or again, violet/fairly bright and light blue/light leaf green/coral/mauve/white, on a yellow ground. Another rarer combination is based on violet/grey/browns/old rose/cream. Later pieces tend to have brighter colours.

In some of the more rustic pieces, the elaborate geometric pattern has simply turned into many coloured squares, usually arranged in chevrons or slanting lines. For some reason these mosaic panels are often more clearly rectangular.

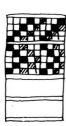

Chéchaouen Figure 2. Especially in the more rustic pieces, the rectangular shape becomes pronounced and may even be pulled out of true.

Rustic embroidery from Chéchaouen, early 20th century

Others, using a completely different technique, are conceived as ribbons of very fine needleweaving, sometimes each band in a different pattern.

(b) This area is made up of two elements — narrow ribbons of polychrome needleweaving and a monochrome background of Rhodian stitch, generally in brick red, or sometimes in deep blue or soft violet. This background is interesting for several reasons. It is generally worked in a squared pattern — each square being known as a *bait* or house — which gives a very rich texture. The stitches, of course, completely cover the ground and may be more or less curly, thus confusing the pattern. This bouclé effect was much prized by the Copts and is to be seen in a number of their textiles. It spread in the wake of the Arab conquests to Sicily and Calabria, Andalusia, the Balearic Islands, and eventually the Balkans and Yugoslavia. Different techniques may be used to obtain this look. In modern Morocco it is worked quite extensively, but in a range of colours and to make designs of baskets of flowers and so on, not as a solid background. A rather loose-weave cotton is chosen and the soft thread is pulled through and twisted with an implement not unlike a fine crochet hook. The stitch is currently known there as Meccan Stitch, Eastern Stitch or Circassian Stitch, suggesting that it came from the East, perhaps with the Turks, relatively recently, rather than with the Andalusians long ago.

The ribbons of needleweaving are often quite fine. This is, incidentally, a favourite Moroccan technique for finishing the edge of a piece of work and may be coloured or monochrome, very rarely with the addition of gold or silver thread.

Detail of fine Chéchaouen piece, showing section (c) with stylized stars

(c) The central element is made up of three stars, one large and two small, surrounded by a star-burst of embroidery. In some of the more rustic examples this may become one star or even just a square. In the large pieces the whole pattern a-b-c-b-a is repeated twice, with a space between; there may also be a star floating in the middle of the field.

The stars themselves are either embroidered in a manner very similar to the mosaic panels and set in surrounds of Rhodian stitch, or else are appliquéd. This second type of star seems to have come into fashion in the mid-19th century and was a speciality of the Jewish women. The stars are cut out of red velvet stretched on a leather backing and richly decorated with gold embroidery and gold sequins. This effect is glittery and striking, but much less subtle than the earlier embroideries. Stars detached from their background, or perhaps never applied, can be found fairly often in the local antique shops and the best ones, on their own, have a very pleasant look of filigree. This kind of Chéchaouen embroidery no longer seems to be done today.

Quite common in the area are long pieces of handwoven linen, said to be women's veils or head coverings, decorated with a very rustic version of the a-b-c-b-a pattern in flat stitch worked in very soft loosely twisted silk floss, of a kind which wears out easily, often in delightfully subtle colours: lavender/rose/cream/grey or soft rose red/grey blue/cream/terracotta. I have never seen them worn, nor being made, nor have I managed to find out anything precise about them. They are not very old, however – perhaps forty years – and would be an excellent thing to revive for sale as scarves and stoles. Again, the colour schemes and designs would be quite quick and easy to copy and are suitable for wool, although it would be wise to choose a shorter and less easily unravelled stitch.

The other pieces of Chéchaouen work are mostly cushion covers, typically worked in Rhodian stitch, either in squares, as described above (b) or in bands of stylized flowers and trees, not dissimilar to those of Fez. The curly stitch has the effect of making the design hard to see, and, incidentally, almost impossible to photograph successfully – altogether a very curious idea.

There are also one or two fine but aberrant examples, in particular one in the museum at Algiers, believed to be Chéchaouen work. They are described by Mme Guérard in her article, but there is not space to discuss them here.

FEZ

Fez is among the most perfectly preserved cities of the Muslim world and one in which it is easy to imagine the life of an earlier age. The beautiful mosques and madrasahs; the narrow streets, barely adequate for horses or mules, let alone cars; the enormous numbers of craftsmen engaged in traditional occupations; and the lack of shoddy, ill-considered Western intrusions, make walking around it a great joy.

According to tradition, Fez was founded in AD 809 by Idriss ibn Abdallah, a descendant of the Prophet via his daughter Fatima, who fled to North Africa to escape the Abbasid persecution. The city has three main divisions – Fez al-Bali, Old Fez; Fez al-Jedid, New Fez, founded in the 13th century; Fez Ville, the French colonial town, largely built early this century.

Fez has always been a royal city with a court and is indeed the oldest of the Moroccan towns known as *makhzen* – imperial. It was rich through trade, both with the coast and southwards into Africa. At various times in its history it welcomed refugees, who brought with them a long cultural tradition and skilled artisans. Among the most notable were those who came from Kairouan in Tunisia in the 10th century (hence the name of the great mosque – Al-Qarawiyyin) and various waves from Andalusia.

Some sources

According to the *Zahra al-As*, in 1069-70, Yusuf ibn Tashfin, the Almoravid reformer and conqueror of Spain, having founded Marrakesh some eight years previously, brought workmen from Cordova to build or restore numerous buildings in Fez. There was also, according to the historian al-Bakri, a flourishing and skilled Jewish community established in a *mellah* next to the Sultan's palace. These factors and those mentioned above served to make Fez a centre for the arts, which were both produced and consumed there – and this is as true of textiles and embroideries as of anything else.

A late 12th or early 13th-century history of Fez tells us:

> "…there were at Fez…467 funduks [storehouses, especially for foreigners]…3094 houses of tiraz [originally these were the official factories of

embroidery or fine weaving]...and 116 dyehouses.
...inside the walls."

It is worth mentioning here that dyeing in the Islamic world was very often a Jewish specialty. There were various reasons for this. It was highly skilled and the Jewish communities have traditionally veered towards the skilled occupations. It was a form of specialized knowledge, like goldsmithing, easily moved from one country to another in times of trouble. Again, the Muslims, intermittently at least, felt that in theory dyeing was altering God's creation and therefore not quite licit. At certain places and at certain times, it was therefore preferred that some other group should undertake it. The same sort of ruling periodically affected other activities such as distilling scent, leavening bread and tattooing.

That there was a considerable trade in clothes and textiles from Fez is well documented and an early reference comes from the Cairo *Geniza*. Although it does not refer specifically to embroideries, it is charming and deserves to be quoted. From Almeria in Spain, December 1141:

> "...buy a silk robe from the master who made the *'attabi* (tabby) for the elder Abu Zikri...It should be tailored. If you cannot get it ready made, have it made quickly. Dye it pistachio green (the colour of Paradise), and have it ironed in the very best way. Send it on quickly with the mats for Abraham, for the robe is also for him and he needs it for his wedding."
>
> Goitein, *Letters,* p.265

Fez fragment, probably of a cushion border, early 19th century

Museums and shops

Fez is still a city with a considerable level of traditional refinement and although weaving, carpet-making and embroidery on leather do not fall within the scope of this book, they can all be observed there. For those interested in embroidery, some of the principal places to visit are the attractive 19th-century palace in the Andalusian manner, the Dar Bartha, now the Museum of Moroccan Art, which has a nice collection of Fez-style embroideries, in particular wall-hangings. There is, in addition, a section for carpets and weaving with some fine belts. Furthermore, the Dar Bartha will advise on visiting the local workshops of any craft, which is useful since some are not self-evident and Fez is a confusing city.

Not to be missed is the very spectacular dyers quarter (where wool is used rather than cotton or silk) near the Madrasa al-Saffarin, which lies by the Fez River. Embroideries, in particular the magnificent gold embroidery for which Fez is famous — the saddles and horse trappings are especially fine — are to be found in the region of the Souk al-Attarin (Scent Souk) and the Qaysariya (elsewhere Kissaria, both from the word *Caesar*) market.

The embroidery

The embroidery of Fez, although arguably limited as regards technique and with patterns which are all very similar in effect, uses some of the most ancient design elements of the Mediterranean, as Mme Jouin has pointed out in her article. (See bibliography.) The fleur-de-lys was a symbol of fertility in Egypt and of royalty in Crete. The eight-pointed star is to be found in Syria in Classical times and throughout the Islamic world. It is often associated with the seal of Solomon, and in Morocco appears over and over again; with the hand it forms the almost invariable border of every woven belt. Stylized vases or lamps were old when the Copts adopted them for their textiles and still form part of the normal repertory for prayer rugs. There are all-over patterns which can be paralleled in Byzantine textiles and even in mosaics. The symbol of the hand is probably one of the oldest in the world. It is sometimes considered to be the Hand of Fatima, the daughter of the Prophet, and in North Africa, as elsewhere in the Islamic world, is popularly believed to have immense prophylactic powers. As an amulet it is to be found everywhere and hand-prints in red or blue paint over the lintel are a common way of providing protection for a house or shop.

Identifiable foreign elements also appear in other aspects of Fez embroidery. The embroidery frame used, for example, is of the

Turkish type – made of wood, rectangular and four-legged, some-times plain and sometimes decorated with mother-of-pearl inlay. The women traditionally worked sitting on the floor, although the frame is now quite often set on a table. This is the standard arrangement in Turkey and is also found in North Africa wherever Turkish influence was particularly strong – as in Algiers, Cairo and Tunis. Fez, unlike the other cities, was not directly under Turkish domination, but it is known that women from that area were imported for use in the harems and presumably they brought their embroidery techniques with them.

The same is true of the stitches used in Fez embroidery. Today, it is all done in counted thread and the basic stitch – Fez Stitch – is a kind of reversible back stitch either worked in steps, or as a version of what the French call "reversible three-sided Turkish stitch". As far as Fez is concerned, it would indeed seem to be Turkish and it has been argued that it is a comparatively recent introduction, since it is not found in the earliest pieces. Another, older, stitch called Aleuj stitch is ultimately of Persian origin and is basic to the embroideries of Janina in the Balkans.

Aleuj embroideries

The word 'aleuj means "one who has converted to Islam" or, in Classical Arabic, simply "alien". Perhaps the meaning arose after some Christian girl imported the style into a Fez household, taught the other women and eventually changed her faith? It is of course impossible to know.

Aleuj embroideries survive from the late 17th century and continue until the very early 19th, when they ceased to be made. There was a not very successful late 19th and early 20th-century revival, which again died out and no aleuj work is attempted today.

Detail of an 'aleuj cushion end – Fez 18th Century.

Aleuj embroideries are much more compact than counted work and non-reversible. The main blocks are done in a kind of slanted satin stitch, with a fine herring-bone stitch to divide the different colours or motifs and back stitch or stem stitch for the outlines. Aleuj pieces are typically monochrome and the narrow lines of background cloth left uncovered by the stitches are what make the pattern (as at Azemmour). The ground is quite often linen, particularly in the earlier pieces, and the favourite colours are carmine, old gold, rust, violet, blue-black, dull green. Sometimes two shades of one colour are used: violet/aubergine or old gold/ brown. Gold thread may also be used, as a rule sparingly. The patterns are basically geometric, but the borders may end with stylized leaves, or the design may include very diagrammatic carnations or four- or eight-petalled flowers.

It seems likely that the original aleuj embroideries were drawn on the cloth freehand, probably by the most skilled of the *ma'alle-ma* (teacher), for they are varied and lively. During the attempt to revive them, a type of wood-block was apparently used to give the outline of the pattern, with a repetitive and hence much duller effect. More recently still, the women of Fez have adopted, for their European-style non-counted-thread embroidery, the French customs of tracing paper and pouncing.

So little is known about aleuj embroideries that it is hard to be sure what they were used for. The pieces which survive today mostly appear to be cushion covers. Fez, however, has always made particular use of cushions and larger worn pieces are often reused in this way, so aleuj embroideries may also have included hangings, and so on.

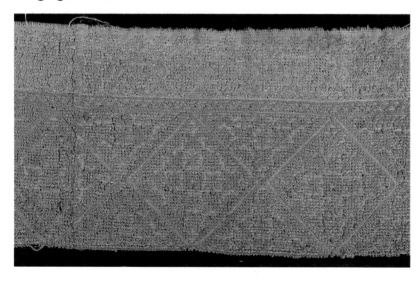

Fez fragment, probably, of a cushion border, 19th century

Fez embroideries

Fez embroidery proper – known in Morocco as *terz d-el-ghorza* – dates from the 18th century and has become the most widespread type of embroidery in Morocco today. It is done without a pattern drawn on the cloth, by counting threads, and is reversible, the design having slightly greater relief on the right side. Traditionally, Fez embroidery is monochrome. A range of colours, always delicate or sober, is to be found in the earlier pieces. Later came a fashion for a sombre dark blue, followed by a deep red which became brighter as time went on and was then in part superseded by a rather violent violet. The ground is almost invariably cotton and the thread is a fine silk often used double or triple. The stitches used are Fez stitch, stem stitch, flat stitch, with as always some variants.

*   *   *

Oh stork! Tak, tak!
She has left her children in their basket
And has gone to hunt partridges.
A sickle has hurt her leg –
"Aisha, my sister,
Give me a little honey,
So I can tend my leg!"
A red thread,
A yellow thread,
A thread all strung with pearls!"

*   *   *

Fez fragment, probably of a cushion border, 19th century

Fez fragment, 19th century. This is on finer material than the three previous examples and was perhaps part of a mendil

The patterns are largely geometric, but the borders tend to end with stylized plants, particularly trees, on which a bird may be perched. This bird is generally identified with the stork, which has some of the same significance as it has for us and is much loved. It is thought to bring good fortune and a stork's nest on one's house is much prized. It is also felt to possess *baraka* – blessing, because so many of them live in holy places and on the minarets of mosques. The trees themselves carry a faint suggestion of palm or cypress – an echo again, perhaps, of the ancient Tree of Life? It is possible also to find vases or pots of flowers, even garlands, but it requires a willing and imaginative eye. The "hand of Fatima" is another common element, as is the eight-pointed star. Modern Fez embroidery tends to be more strictly geometric and it is rare to find the long elaborate borders of alternating "flowers" and "trees".

This type of embroidery does not appear to have been much used at Fez for clothing, although the occasional sash for securing the *sarwal* – or women's trousers – may be found. There were also *merbet* (pl. *mrabet*), a kind of pleated gaiter reaching from knee to ankle and fastened at the side by loops and buttons. They used to be worn by Fezzi women in the street, but have long since been replaced by stockings or socks. It is also possible that some of the less stiff rectangular pieces were intended as *derra*, or scarves.

*   *   *

Who can know how the dawn will break after the
night?
Clove carnation and jasmine are wed, the rose
has bloomed,
For us, my cousin [m] and I, lying on one mattress.

*   *   *

The principal domestic items are *telmita* – mattress covers, and *tlamt d-el khrib* – strips about 3 m × 75 cm, intended to hide the side of the mattress. These may seem a curious idea to us, but they are in fact common items of folk embroidery in a number of countries, for example throughout Northern Europe, or again China, where the finest surviving examples of blue and white peasant embroidery are bed valances, designed to hide the side of the mattress and the underside of the bed. The Fez pieces date from the 18th and earlier part of the 19th century and are worked in an all-over diamond pattern, each diamond containing a stylized flower or star, which may look like an ice crystal. The network making up the diamonds may be composed of crossed crosses
forming or suggesting further diamonds; to my mind this, together with the *mendil el-mjamar* (see over), is Fez work at its best. The patterns echo those of the coffered wood ceilings, the elaborate carved doors and the plaster-work of the great houses, which so clearly trace their style back to the Hispano-Mauresque.

*   *   *

"A neat bed is better than a messy husband."
Fez Proverb

*   *   *

These pieces are most commonly dark blue, although greyish violet, aubergine and very dark green are also found. Interestingly, although the embroidery went out of use a century ago, the patterns are still common ones printed on mattress ticking in Morocco today. It is rare to find a complete mattress cover, but little scraps are very easily bought. They have often been mounted into small bags, pouches or wallets, which are not necessarily new. In Rabat, for example, I saw a piece decorating a leather case for carrying a prayer book; it had apparently been reused in this way around the turn of the century.

Detail of a Fez mattress cover, early 19th century. This work, which is very thick and raised, is quite indestructible

In Fez, as in other cities in Morocco, embroidered curtains or hangings are quite common. The ground is usually very heavily

Motif from a "brazier cloth" – Fez.

worked, sometimes all over, and the commonest colour is red followed by violet. Fez hangings tend to be somewhat smaller than those of Rabat, they do not have the curious dividing strip, and pieces apparently intended to be single hangings, rather than pairs, occur.

Another very fine, but rare, group of Fez embroideries is that of the *mendil el-mjamar* or Brazier Cloths – so-called because in the rather random way, so common around the Mediterranean, the bunches of flowers scattered over them were thought to look like braziers. The cloths were in fact used for wrapping up packets of clothes. *Mendil*, or square cloths, often richly decorated, were basic items of elegance all over the Muslim Mediterranean. They, like the Japanese *furoshiki*, were part of the equipment for going to the *hammam*, or Turkish bath and, again like the *furoshiki*, were used as carrying cloths, by knotting the corners together, or for presenting formal gifts. Precious objects would be put away wrapped in them, they might be used to cover a tray of tea or cakes, or spread on the lap of a bride during the elaborate hennaing of her hands – often, incidentally, in patterns which recall the embroideries themselves.

These cloths are roughly square, approximately 1.40 m × 1.60 m, and embroidered on a plain cotton ground in one or two shades – deep blue/violet, mauve/old rose, darker and lighter grey blue being typical combinations. The design radiates out from a central star in an arrangement which recalls some of the pieces from Meknès. The star may be enclosed in a diamond, a lobed pattern or another star. Eight lines join the star to the corners and the centres of the sides. The eight triangles thus obtained are filled with fairly regularly arranged smaller stars, or very stylized flower sprigs. Each piece is quite individual and has its own charm. They date from the late 18th to the mid-19th centuries, when for some reason they ceased to be made.

By far the most common type of Fez embroidery is that described at the beginning – geometric or stylized plant motifs arranged in bands, sometimes so as to cover large areas, and often ending with a line of plants or trees. This work appears around the edge of the *mendil*, or cloths, on the cushions for which Fez was particularly well-known (it should be remembered that older and larger pieces are often reused as cushion covers and that this has been going on for a long time) and, occasionally, hangings. The cushions which are completely covered with embroidery are known as *mhedda* (pl *mhadd*). They may either be large rectangles or else a kind of long thin bolster shape. They were a basic item of furniture and decoration and a row of them along the couches which ran around three sides of the sitting room were an essential part of any well-to-do home. There are also "pillow slips" with only a little embroidery at the ends which were used to protect the cushions on occasions when they were going to be slept on. Lastly there is the specifically Fezzi object, the *gelsa*, a square napkin used to mark the places intended for the guests of honour on the divans of the *majlis*, or reception room.

Detail of a particularly elegant Fez bed-spread, late 18th or early 19th century. Note the rather complicated and somewhat European-looking border

GOLD EMBROIDERIES OF FEZ

Organization and techniques

Gold embroidery – *terz d-es-sqalli*, perhaps meaning Sicilian – is not exclusive to Fez. It is done in urban centres all over Morocco, and indeed all over North Africa, but that of Fez is particularly famous and the areas of the souk where gold embroidery is sold are among the most spectacular. Much of what is said below holds true generally – even in Libya, where very little embroidery is done, since it is quite firmly a weaving culture. It is made only in a few cities and is done in silk and gold, primarily on leather.

The organization of the embroideresses working with gold or silver thread is similar to that of those using silk. In the past they never belonged to the guilds or corporations, nor dealt directly with their patrons. The former still holds and the latter seems to be truer of gold embroidery than of silk, presumably because more of the clients are men. As a rule, women do the embroidery on cloth and men the harder work on leather. Similarly, it is men who do the finishing – sewing together pouches, making up slippers, and so on.

Every aspect of gold embroidery at Fez was admirably researched and documented by A.M.Goichon in 1939 and much of what he says holds today. At that date, work was still paid by weight, but the amount of time it would take to use up an ounce of thread naturally depended on the type of design. "For a *kiswa* – veil for the tomb of a marabout (saint) – decorated with bands of large embroidered letters... it is quickly used up, in roughly four days; but for slippers with a dense and delicate pattern, which is difficult to work, it takes a good week to use up an ounce."

It is always very hard to estimate the number of workers in a situation where most of them operate at home, often part-time, and there are no guild registers, but A.M. Goichon was given the figures of 2,000 women embroidering in silk thread and 2,500 in gold. Forty years later, I was told that the number was less than half – but this was, I think, a guess, not the result of any statistical survey.

Besides embroiderers, there were others, both men and women, who made all the various kinds of braids, tassels and trimmings known as *mjadli*.

Oh you who walk along the ramparts,
Ramparts pierced everywhere with arrow slits,
Behold Mansur –
Oh silken trimming of a caftan's edge!

*   *   *

Gold and silver embroidery is typically done on velvet or leather. There are a number of different qualities of thread available, real gold obviously now being extremely rare. Until the early part of this century, making the thread was – as were most kinds of work involving precious metals – the speciality of the Jews in the *mellah*. Now it is quite often imported, or made industrially in Morocco. The technique used for working it is always couching – that is, the metal thread is never passed through the material to the reverse side. The thread used for the small stitches which hold the metal in place was traditionally a strong linen known as *hit susi* – originally from Sousse in Tunisia.

The patterns are drawn by the artisans (and then given to the women), in paper for slippers and thin leather for the larger pieces, and then cut out. Each design has a name. A circle, no matter what it has inside, is *teffaha* – apple. Flowers are by definition *yasmina* – jasmin. Tear drops are *mressa* – a vase for sprinkling rose water. An oval with veined markings is *guza* – walnut, while squares and lozenges are invariably *zellij* – tile.

Clothing

The shops selling gold embroideries today look like something out of the Arabian Nights. In the past, the velvets used were generally dark – black, wine, bottle green, dark blue, violet – but recently taste has become broader and there are rows of slippers and mules in every imaginable shade, especially those mentioned above, but apple green, cerise, pale blue, white and rose are also favourites. Their effect is extraordinarily attractive. Besides these slippers (respectable young women, I have been told do not wear them in the street, at least in Fez, although old ladies may), the commonest pieces are belts, always objects of great importance in North Africa and ones to which a great deal of symbolic importance is attached. It was customary for a well-to-do Fez girl to have at least one in her dowry, which might be anything ranging from a simple velvet band with a little decoration fastened with a hook to an extremely fine and delicate example of craftsmanship, where the ground is entirely covered and the clasp, sold separately, is of

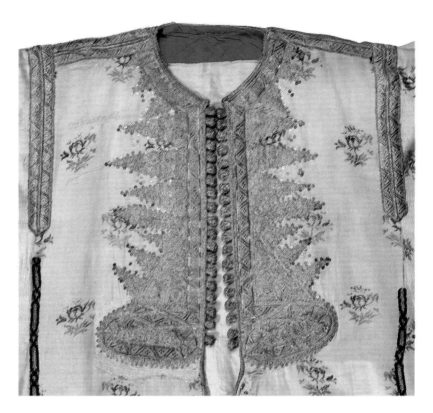

Man's Moroccan robe, (acquired in Tangiers), 19th century. The silk is certainly European, probably French. The style purely Turkish – see facing plate

wrought silver or gold. This fashion has now spread throughout Morocco. Prices vary immensely, but in 1981 the slippers sold commonly in Fez ranged from £6-£20, while the belts were roughly £10-£50. Obviously much more expensive pieces could be commissioned, and apparently quite often are. At the other end of the scale, very inexpensive but pretty belts are made with self-coloured or neutral embroidery on the same range of velvets, using much the same designs as for the gold belts, but worked in satin stitch.

Other items include children's clothes. Girls have belts and slippers which are miniatures of their mothers'. For boys, there are circumcision costumes, although, apart from a velvet fez or tarbush – usually dark green, dark blue or purple with a design of garlands and the crescent moon – these are rarely seen offered for sale in Morocco. Presumably they are made at home, ordered specially, or rented for the occasion. In Fez, the circumcision costume generally consisted of a gold embroidered velvet burnous to match the fez. In other parts of North Africa, a "Turkish-style" costume of jacket and wide trousers is preferred – and, of course, fashions change.

Young man's Turkish robe, early 19th century

This year (1983), for example, I noticed that in Istanbul the preferred colour was sky blue, followed by ivory, and that nearly all the boys wore a sash across their chests over their cloaks with the word *"mashallah"* — God's will be done — pasted on in gold letters. In the past it would certainly have been embroidered. In Tunisia, on the other hand, at a double circumcision in Sousse, one little boy wore a dark blue Turkish costume and carried a gold sequin-embroidered good-luck fish, while the other was in a white European suit with a bow tie. They rode a magnificently caparisoned horse with embroidered saddle and saddle cloth, gold anklets on its ears and a yellow wool woman's belt wound three times round its neck. The circumcision ceremony in Tunis and the costume, including the embroideries, have been described by N. Mahjoub (see bibliography).

*   *   *

The striped caftan
Came from the land of the Christians.
A party without Zubeida
In this world is purest loss.

*   *   *

Still on the subject of clothes, it should be mentioned that the magnificent caftans, often made of the most sumptuous and richly coloured imported silks and brocades, and worn by both men and women, were normally finished off with elaborate gold braiding and embroidery, as wedding and evening caftans still are today. These splendid robes are almost indistinguishable from their Turkish counterparts and looking at them, one cannot help being reminded of the words of the Flemish ambassador to Istanbul in 1555, Ogier de Busbecq, who had a very strong preference for Oriental rather than Western dress:

"Look at these marvellously handsome dresses of every kind and every colour; time would fail for me to tell how all around is glittering with gold, with silver, with purple, with silk, with velvet; words cannot convey an adequate idea of that strange and wondrous sight: it was the most beautiful spectacle that ever I saw.

"They were quite as much surprised at our manner of dressing as we were at theirs. They use long robes reaching down to the ankles, which have a stately effect and add to the wearer's height, while our dress is so scanty and short that it leaves to view more than is comely of the human shape; besides, somehow or other, our fashion of dress seems to take from the wearer's height, and make him look shorter than he really is."

Miscellaneous pieces

Other objects worked with gold thread are bags and pouches – some of them probably intended as Koran cases; they certainly were in the past – and texts from the Koran meant for framing to hang on the wall. The lines of gold calligraphy shining against the dark background are particularly splendid; the paler colours are not used for these, excepting the bright strong green which is the prerogative of the *sharifs*, the descendants of Muhammad.

Cushions were also worked in gold thread, either on leather, or velvet. The latter are very fine and extremely expensive and today would almost certainly have to be commissioned specially.

Hiti

Ahmad Hamdan, oh myrtle bough!
Oh bamboo stem! Oh light that fires my heart!
For you I want wall-hangings rich with gold,
Couches and cushions of silk, where you will pass
The nights lying on my breast.

Some of the largest pieces of gold embroidery are the *hiti* (also *hayti*, pl. *hyati*) or wall-hangings used both in the houses and the tents of the wealthy. There is a long tradition of them in Morocco, for one of the early references we have to embroidery in North Africa describes the palace of Mansur at Marrakesh around 1578-93:

> "One of the secretaries said: Curtains most beauti-
> fully worked and embroidered with gold were made
> there and called by the Arabs *hayti*."

The design of a *hiti* is always a series of arches, taking up almost the entire height, to which may be added additional decorations – flowers, arabesques, and so on. They are either embroidered in gold on velvet – these are often very magnificent – or are made by appliqué using two or more colours, red and green being the favourites. These are, I think, more recent and certainly much cheaper. Embroidered *hitis* would always have been made to order – A.M. Goichon mentions a particularly fine one commissioned by the *qadi* of Casablanca. The appliquéd *hitis* may be trimmed with braid or gold thread along the arches. They are often of satin or sometimes of a kind of thin felt. I have one of the latter kind in the rather sugary colours of Modern Rabat embroidery – mid-blue and quite bright pink, with touches of almond green and yellow. The gold embroidered *hiti* were often made in separate panels by the *ma'allema* and then assembled afterwards.

Classic design for a Moroccan hiti *– arches below, "crenellations" above. The latter motif is also found on ceremonial tents. At the base of each arch "swallow's wings".*

Hiti were, and still are, insofar as they are used today, luxury objects. Most families would not possess one, but would hire them on important occasions from a *neggafa* – or mistress of ceremonies, or even, in a poor area, through the local go-between.

They are not entirely secular. The walls of mosques are often decorated with them. Sometimes, particularly in Tunisia, they are beautifully woven of very fine matting in red, green and natural straw – those of the Nabeul region are famous – and may even have calligraphic inscriptions. They are also to be found in the *qubbas* ("cupolas") or tombs of *marabouts*, the holy men, or saints.

Kiswa

The word *kiswa* means "covering" and is applied particularly to the black curtains heavily embroidered with Koranic inscriptions in gold which cover the sacred Ka'aba at Mecca and which are renewed annually. Currently, they are embroidered in Egypt. Pieces of this *kiswa* are highly prized as relics and the poetic name for the ceremony "the veiling of the bride" gives an idea of the strength of the symbolism that underlies it.

Kiswa is also the word for the veils used in North Africa to cover the tombs of the *marabouts*. Often they too are made of appliqué – white on green being a favourite combination, especially if the holy man was a *sharif*, or descendant of Muhammad. In any case there is a tendency towards light on dark. As with the *hitis*, the older and more splendid ones were gold on velvet. In either case, the workmanship is different from that of most of the other pieces we have described, since they were intended to be seen at a certain distance and to provide as magnificent effect as possible, often in a candle- or lamp-lit twilight. The *kiswa* are sometimes decorated with the arch pattern, but generally they have bands of large calligraphy, embroidered rather heavily. Typical phrases are the *shahadah* or Profession of Faith: "There is no god but God; Muhammad is His Prophet", or the opening verses of the Koran known as *al-fatiha* – the Opening: "Praise be to God, Lord of the Worlds."

There is a particularly magnificent 18th-century tomb cover, believed to be from Morocco, or possibly Algeria, in the Musée des Arts Africains et Océaniens at Paris. It is of dark carmine silk embroidered with gilded silver thread and provides an anthology of calligraphic motifs – pious phrases worked into stars, crescents, circles, daisies, squares and cartouches, interspersed with hands of Fatima. The couching is done over very long threads and at a distance looks like weaving.

Tomb covers are a widespread Mediterranean custom, although the type described above most probably reached North Africa from Turkey. In Spain, at All Hallows, it was usual to decorate the tombs with carpets and embroideries, sometimes worked with symbols of the Passion and Pauline Johnstone, in her most interesting work on church embroidery, describes some very splendid ones from Rumania and Russia. There, for people of sufficient importance, portrait tomb covers were made, analogous to the paintings on the lids of Romano-Egyptian coffins – except, of course, that the tomb covers were not buried. Sometimes the figure is shown dead, a *gisant*, as in the case of Maria of Mangop, the second wife of Stephen the Great of Moldavia, who died in 1477, at other times very much alive – for example Tudosca, wife of Basil Lupu, and her son John, both embroidered wearing splendid Turkish-style costume in the mid-17th century. Again, there is a pair done of two brothers, one alive and one dead.

Horse trappings

Undoubtedly the most spectacular pieces to be offered for sale in the normal way are the embroidered saddles, several of which can usually be found at any one time in the major souks, although, because of the slowness of the turnover, they too are often made to order. For this reason, the work is usually done by more than one embroideress, since saddle cloth, saddle in its embroidered cover, reins, girths, etc. would take two or three months of full time work, the saddle cloth alone requiring at least twenty days. Embroidering the saddles in particular is very hard work and ruins the hands and, like most leather embroidery in North Africa, is often done by men.

The finest pieces are generally bought by tribesmen and can be seen in use on festival occasions, or at a fantasia or *jerid* – a display of horsemanship which amounts to a mock battle charge. A.M. Goichon tells us that in 1936 the tribes of Tadla alone bought 1,000 sets of horse trappings – the figure today would be substantially less, although, if a way to export them could be found, I should have thought they might be much appreciated in the Gulf. He also mentions that fashion was of the greatest importance – and the saddlers were always trying to stimulate custom by producing some new and tempting look. Wealthy men would then sell off their old, and perhaps somewhat worn, trappings to buy the latest model. Very used saddles, often after several owners, would sometimes be bought back by the saddler who would then burn the gold work in order to retrieve the metal.

Fashions change a good deal. The older pieces tend to be lightly and delicately worked with very fine designs, but the desire to show off more gold than one's neighbour has caused mid-20th century trappings to be more heavily encrusted, brighter but coarser. Colours also go by fashion. On my visits in the late 70s and early 80s all the examples I happened to see for sale were violet or dark blue. Dark colours are, in fact, generally preferred, partly because they show up the gold better and partly because lighter colours are felt to be a decoration in themselves. There does not appear to be any idea that light colours are in some way feminine, nor that they would get dirty easily, since orange, red, pink and pale blue are not unknown and white and gold is a particularly approved and recognized combination.

Although not strictly part of trappings, it should not be forgotten that in the past an elegant man would also have wanted belts, pouches for powder, sheaths for daggers and swords, and even boots worked in the same way, and that it was the Turkish tradition, no doubt imported by the Janissaries, to spend inordinate sums on all details of clothing and equipment. The Islamic prohibition on men (not women) wearing, or even using, silk and gold has almost never been generally observed, but still it is worth mentioning that armaments and accoutrements were traditionally considered exempt.

MEKNÈS

Meknès takes its name from the great Berber tribe, the Meknes-sa, who, at an uncertain date before the year AD 1000, founded the present city of Meknessa ez Zeitoun – Meknès of the Olive Trees. It is about 28 km from Volubilis, one of the most important Roman cities of Western North Africa. Meknès has had an extremely tempestuous history, but one comparatively free of foreign influence until this century. Many of its monuments were built by the indefatigable Sultan Moulay Ismail (1672-1727), who also spent a certain amount of time trying to marry Louis XIV's daughter by Louise de la Vallière. Unfortunately, this remarkable union never took place, although the Sultan's contact with the French court seems to have affected his architectural ambitions. His building activities included vast palaces and part of the splendid walls, and the great gate known as Bab Manseur al-Aleuj – the Gate of Mansur the Renegade (presumably the architect); tradition has it that the work was carried out by Christian slaves.

*   *   *

The camomile flowers open on the tower,
Beside them the high room, the staircase and the
house.
Two thousand renegades come and go before
your eyes
And two thousand birds make their sweet voices
heard,
But only their Master (God) holds and knows
the heart.

*   *   *

Anyone in Meknès interested in embroidery should visit the Dar Jamai. Not far from the Bab Mansur el-Aleuj, it is a charming place in the Andalusian manner which now houses a very pleasant and representative collection of Moroccan arts and crafts (especially Meknès and Fez), including embroideries. Meknès still has an active production of gold embroidery and in particular of embroidery on leather, which is to be found in the Souk es-Sabbat around the Great Mosque, and to some extent near the Bab Berrima and towards the old *mellah*, or former Jewish quarter. Near Bab Tizimi, there is an institution where orphans are taught to embroider and weave carpets, and their products may be bought. There is also the Dar al-Mansur (near the Jama ez-Zitouna — the Mosque of the Olive), the house of a well-to-do 19th-century merchant, now turned into a tea-room and a shop for souvenirs, including some modern embroideries.

The embroidery

Unfortunately rather little is known about the embroideries of Meknès. There are not many pieces in museums and indeed there seem to be far fewer examples available than of, say, Fez or Rabat. This is probably one reason why they have been much less studied. There is no very obvious reason why there should be fewer pieces from Meknès than elsewhere. Meknès is a much larger city than Azemmour or Chéchaouen (always assuming that Chéchaouen work really does come from there) and, although it has had a fairly colourful history with its share of war and destruction, this is true of many other places in North Africa. Again, it was rich, a royal city, it had a very definite local culture and its embroideries are not particularly fragile. Perhaps the relative lack of foreign intervention meant that Meknès inclined more towards weaving, which is in any case much more deeply rooted in North Africa and especially wherever Berber culture predominates, as we have observed elsewhere. Or, possibly, it is simply chance that the people of Meknès have tended to hold on to their old things and so not many have made their way on to the market.

It is difficult to date Meknès work since so little is known about it, but for the most part it seems to be 19th-century, although the odd piece may go back to the late 18th. Again, it is a city which appears to have lost its embroidery tradition early and little seems to have been produced after 1900. P. Ricard, writing in 1918, says that *terz meknassi*, or Meknès embroidery, was "en crise", swamped by the Fez style "which they learn to work in a passable manner, but alter completely by an extraordinary orgy of colours in the most violent combinations. The Mellah also seems to have given rise to a new and equally strident style...I hope the fashion will not last long."

Ironically, the immediate cause of this was undoubtedly the French drive to revive Moroccan arts and crafts, which was launched during World War I. Exceedingly laudable in that it did provide by then much needed training schools, and so generally raised standards, and saved a number of skills from extinction by providing outlets, it incidentally had the adverse effect of flattening out

local styles less adapted to cottage mass-production.

Meknès embroidery is traditionally done on a very nice white muslin, rather fine (20-25 threads to the centimetre) and striped or checked, or woven with spots or little scattered squares. This adds liveliness to the work, which is in any case not really counted thread, the woven design being enough to provide a guide line, and hence much less cold and mechanical than the later Fez work. A range of straight and flat stitches are used, including those of Fez, the embroideresses of Meknès being fairly eclectic, but basically there are darning and running stitches, worked in squares, diagonals, or

Child's (or conceivably young bride's) qamise-chemise- from Meknès. Both colour scheme and design are absolutely typical, but the work is particularly fine. Probably early 19th century

in some version of the favourite step motif.

For some reason, square pieces are the most common and there is a taste for a central square with lines radiating out from it to make a kind of star, rather in the manner of the *mendil el-mjamar* – "brazier cloths" of Fez. The background is usually quite densely covered with embroidered spots and squares, which as a rule do not coincide with the woven ones, giving a pleasant and eccentric effect. There are also rectangular pieces with heavy borders, generally called *sau* or bath veils, probably used for tying up the hair. They were part of a well-to-do woman's elegant equipment for going to the *hammam* – there were relatively few occasions to show off one's possessions and this was one of them, hence the great care lavished on all toilette articles. The border patterns are again not dissimilar to those of Fez, but the main ground has the usual spots or squares. Women's belts are also to be found and occasional fragments of what may have been hangings – a complete one is to be seen displayed in the Dar Jamai Museum.

The Whitworth Museum in Manchester has an especially nice piece. It appears to be either a child's robe or conceivably, although the neck opening is very small, a wedding *qamis* or tunic. It is more or less square in shape, with the traditional square and star design worked in comparatively soft colours: mauve/wine/green/yellow over a printed pattern of pink "roses". The effect is rich and strange. The tunic is open on the right shoulder and down the sides, with tassels, buttons of needlework and loops.

The colours used at Meknès are warm and reminiscent of the kelims of the Berber country, and the effect depends more on colour than design. Red, often dark, tends to predominate, then orange, yellow, brown, black and occasionally green. The blue/violet/grey range is rare. Often a motif will be worked half in one colour, half in another and outlined in black or brown stem stitch. Pastel effects are unknown.

Since P. Ricard was already having trouble finding embroideresses doing the traditional work before 1918, it is hardly surprising that I failed in 1981. This does not mean, however, that there is not the occasional woman who still does it for her own pleasure. And there is always the hope that one day the official Artisanat service will think it worth reviving.

One small proof of its existence in the not so distant past – a very faded board painted with a stylized bride covered with jewels and, written round her in a rather untutored hand, the information that such and such a lady, a *hajjiya* (one who has made the pilgrimage to Mecca and hence an especially respectable and auspicious personage) was available to help prepare trousseaux in the Meknès or Fez manner and was also expert in decorating the bridal chamber. It was quite possible that she would also have had wedding dresses, hangings, and so on to rent to her clients, since it was a poor quarter of town where few could have possessed the more expensive items. These boards, incidentally, are a charming and now very rare feature of Moroccan towns and provided a way for a woman of a certain age to advertise her skills – pastry cook, dressmaker, embroideress; and sometimes she would also be the local *dallala*, "guide" or go-between (cognate with the name Dalilah) and so earn her living.

* * *

God divided beauty and ten carried it away.
Soap, henna and silk – there are three.
The plough, the flocks, the swarms of bees –
That's six.
The sun when it rises on the mountain tops –
That's seven.
The crescent moon, thin as a Christian's knife –
That's eight.
With horses and with books we have reached
ten.
And the Prophet Muhammad, the Messenger,
Has taken all the rest.

* * *

RABAT

The site of Rabat seems to have been a Phoenician and Carthaginian trading post, and later a classical city – in fact this, rather than Salé, may have been the site of Salacolonia, afterwards known as Solga.

In the 8th century, a *ribat* or fortress of men dedicated to *jihad* or holy war (they had a good deal in common with the Christian orders of knights) was established, probably where the kasba now stands, overlooking the Bou Regreg river. Later, when the wars against the Berbers were at an end, it served as a launching point for the incursions into Spain.

The city as it is today was founded at the very end of the 12th century by Abu Yusuf Yaqub al-Mansur and, like so many Arab cities, it was given both name and epithet: Ribat al-Fath – Rabat of Victory. It was al-Mansur who likewise began the great mosque which remained unfinished, although its minaret, the Tour Hassan, sister to that of the Zeituna Mosque at Tunis and the Giralda in Seville, is a landmark to this day. Its name is, incidentally, some-times given to the *tala* or minaret-shaped embroideries up the seams of the larger Rabat hangings. The Hassan Mosque was planned to be the biggest in the Islamic world after the Friday Mosque at Samarra in Iraq.

In 1609 Rabat received a large contingent of refugees from Spain, in particular from Hornachos in the province of Badajoz. Quarrels between these different groups were now added to all of Morocco's other wars.

From this time on, Rabat's main *raison d'être* was piracy and, through captured prisoners and voluntary renegades, the city had a moderately cosmopolitan character. As at Salé, seamen from all over Europe – Jan Janssen of Haarlem, who became Morat Raïs, or the renegade Englishman who had the mosque of the kasba restored, are only two of many – came to Rabat to seek their fortune, often by raiding their own countries and countrymen. The captured cannons in the Kasba al-Oudaïa bear witness to their success.

For those interested in embroidery, there is, just near the kasba, the Museum of Islamic Arts, with some nice pieces of Rabat embroidery, a few examples from Fez, and one or two things from Tétouan and Salé, not, unfortunately, labelled. Almost opposite, there is the new Centre of Artisanat (Arts and Crafts), where it is often possible to see demonstrations of modern embroidery done by the girls being trained in one of the official schemes. These state trainees numbered 1,500-2,000 in various parts of the country in 1983. (The imprecision is mine, not that of the Moroccan authorities, to whom I apologize.) It is possible to buy a very attractive selection of their work on the spot. There is also a carpet-making establishment nearby.

In the small streets of the Medina, especially in the neighbourhood of Rue Bou Kroun, there are numerous little embroidery shops and workshops, as at Salé.

Rabat was – and is – a great city for embroidery. Ever since the refugees from Andulasia settled there in the early 17th century, it seems to have produced large quantities of embroideries, both furnishings and clothes. The style has, however, changed more than once.

Old Rabati embroideries

Already in the Middle Ages, Salé was called a "mine of cotton and linen" and Leo Africanus praised its weaving, but Rabat is not mentioned, although the first extant Rabati embroideries date back to the early 18th or possibly even very late 17th century. The background material is generally white or natural cotton, sometimes checked or striped or damasked. The silk thread used was soft, locally made and dyed with vegetable colours to give beautiful soft gradations of tone. Often, even in a piece of work theoretically of one colour, there will be a number of different shades, owing to irregularities in the dyeing, which give a particular richness and life to the work. One of the problems with industrial thread is that the colours match too perfectly and so this effect is lost. With skill, it can be recovered artificially by slight gradations of shade instead of a single colour chart number.

The preferred colours of Old Rabati Work are carmine, deep blue and old gold; the red, as usual, predominating. Again, in these pieces, the pattern appears not to have been drawn, but outlined by a free-hand row of stitches which the embroidery then covers. This would have required considerable skill, although, as at Meknès, the patterned material would have helped to orientate the design. The work is not reversible and the favourite stitches are chain, an elongated form of button-hole and darning stitch, with other stitches such as seed stitch for odd details. It seems likely that this Rabat work was done on a tightly stuffed cushion (as opposed to an embroidery frame) of the type still in use at the beginning of the century. These early pieces are generally fragmentary and may be monochrome or polychrome; in the latter case only one colour is normally used for each design element.

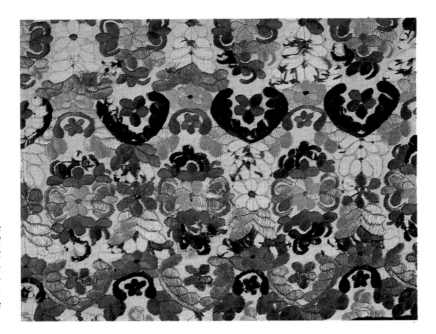

Rabat cushion cover, late 19th century. This detail shows how the soft silk floss tends to wear out revealing the freehand pattern drawn on the cloth. The colour scheme is one of Rabat's favourites

Corner of a cushion from Rabat with the first of a row of figures embroidered in deep red silk. They are not considered to be "brides" since the motif probably originated with the ladies in Renaissance dress on laces etc., from Venice.

The most common pattern, dating from the late 18th to the early-mid 19th century, is that of a row of little figures, very stylized, with a round head and a full skirt, of the kind described for Azemmour. They are usually rather heavily embroidered and stand on a solid border often with a zig-zag pattern. Rudimentary arms are shown, sometimes with an indication that they are raised in the archaic position of supplication or prayer. Very formal leaves or flowers may sprout from the skirt. The ground above the border of figures is generally scattered with embroidered squares, sprays of flowers stylized into squares, as at Meknès, or simply very rigid floral motifs. Frequently the figures too are so schematic as to be barely recognizable and indeed were called by the embroideresses *sraref* or crenellations, or they might lean, as a rule to the left, to become *khinjar*, or daggers.

*   *   *

Embroideress, embroideress,
Embroider me a cap
To give to Mustafa, when on his wedding day
He enters the bridal chamber.

*   *   *

Another type of pattern considered by Mme Brunot-David and Mme Guérard to be earlier, perhaps late 17th or early 18th century, is made up essentially of squares, crosses and curlicues, or else of oval forms filled with curlicues. It is extremely rare and I have only seen one or two pieces in museums. Little is known about it, although Mme Brunot-David writes that "in spite of lack of documentation, they make one think of the old embroidery on the Spanish waistcoats from Extremadura, Lagartera and Castille." This is perfectly true. They also seem to have points in common with the embroidery (really braiding and frogging) still done today on men's robes in North Africa, particularly those of Tunis, and also with the patterns sometimes worked on boys' circumcision outfits. But this is an aspect that would need further study.

Another design, of which Mme Guérard has found only a single example, which she dates to the late 17th or early 18th century, is worth mentioning, because it could be the ultimate development of the little rows of figures, or else a completely different pattern: a row of domes – the *qubbas* or tombs of saints, perhaps? – or pavilions, very faintly reminiscent of those so popular in Turkish embroidery. Here each "house" is in red, blue or yellow, with the first colour predominating.

The last category of Old Rabat embroidery is that of stylized floral designs and it is from this kind of work that all the later 19th- and early 20th-century embroideries seem to derive.

When the figures, again embroidered in lines of flat stitch, lean over, they are called khinjar – dagger – *Rabat cushion.*

Rabat fragments, perhaps of a hanging, pieced together to make a cover for a chest or something similar. The elaborate fringe similar to that on p.59 is not shown. First half of the 20th century

Again, there are two types. The most common has rather bold and very formalized plant motifs, relatively large, worked in thick soft silk in what is almost satin stitch, with a good deal of ground showing between the "petals" or "leaves". They have beautiful colours in a very wide range — for example, shades of pale and grey blue/mauve/wine/ivory/pale apple and moss green/carmine, with touches of yellow; or, more simply coral/grey-blue/garnet, with touches of other colours. This last was the colour scheme of a particular small hanging called *tobaza*, which measures approximately 1.25 cm in height by 40 cm in width. According to Mme Guérard it was a piece of decoration used exclusively by the Jews, in particular for wedding ceremonies, but it was made by Muslim embroideresses. The question of which group made which pieces seems insoluble at this late date. In Morocco itself I was told all sorts of conflicting stories — that Rabati curtains were made exclusively by Jews for use by Muslims, and also that they were made exclusively by Muslims for use by Jews — all of which may have been true in a particular place and at a particular time.

The other style, of which I have seen only one example, appears, curiously enough, to be the ancestor of a great deal of modern embroidery, some, in the earlier part of this century, done by hand, but now almost always worked by machine. Its characteristics are smaller, tighter stitches than the other type, with a more precise design and more delicate colours — in the one 18th-century example I have seen, pale mauve/pale and mid blue/almond green/ivory/pale yellow/gold/faded carmine/aubergine — in the modern pieces a rather sugary, though pretty, pastel range is used.

These pieces are all hangings or parts of hangings, although bed-decorations, cushions and possibly certain articles of clothing were made in the same way.

"Allah" embroidered in yellow and red on the green leather cover of a prayer book — Rabat 19th century.

New Rabat embroidery

From the mid-19th century all the styles we have mentioned above, except the floral, went out of fashion and with them the non-reversible stitches. The patterns were now drawn on to the background material by a *ma'allema* who was particularly skilled and an enormous range of variants both in shape and colour was produced with relatively few elements. These have, by the way, been admirably analyzed by P. Ricard. He also gives his theory of how the designs came into being and provides useful vocabulary:

"It is the mistress-embroideress (*mallema reqqama*) who marks (*tekteb*) the outline of the design (*kitaba*) to be executed on the material with a pencil (*lapiz*). Apprentices or hired girls then begin to embroider (*rqem*) the pieces which have already been drawn."

Curtains

This was the period at which the most characteristic Rabat pieces were made – the great *izar* (pl. *izur*) or curtains, often about 4 m long and 2-3 m wide. Hung as decorations on ceremonial occasions, they were things that only the richer families would possess, although they were often borrowed or hired for a wedding or festival. Owning such pieces was, as elsewhere in Morocco, and indeed all round the Mediterranean, a source of pride and often they would be among the most important items officially enumerated in the dowry. An analogous position is still held in rural Tunisia by woven hangings, and in Algeria last century and early this by embroidered ones.

The same was true until early last century in the Greek Islands of the *sparvers* or bed tents, although they were hung in a completely different way from those of North Africa. Circular and narrower at the top than the bottom, they resemble those of Renaissance Italy, from which they probably derived. In Turkey, these large marriage curtains do not seem to have been standard, although embroidered curtains exist, conceivably because the arrangement of the rooms allowed more privacy than was the norm in even a well-to-do North African home. It was, however, and to a limited extent still is, the custom to decorate the bride bed and the circumcision bed with as much fine embroidery as the family could manage. In all these cases the idea was, of course, to decorate, to provide a special atmosphere for a special occasion, to protect with lucky symbols, embroidered, painted or woven, but also to display the wealth of the family and the skill and taste of its women. Not to be able to embroider in the Greek Islands up until the last century, like not being able to weave in many areas of Tunisia until relatively recently, was considered shaming. The same was doubtless true of Morocco, although there is little direct evidence as to whether the finest pieces were the work of paid professionals, or the *ma'allema*-trained daughters of the house. The quality would in any case have been similar. Naturally, in times of financial need, these good pieces would, regretfully, have been sold (although in some of the Greek islands it was possible to borrow money against them), usually at a very poor price, through a *dallala* or broker.

Rabat curtains have great charm and are, as they were meant to

Pair of Rabat marriage curtains embroidered in soft silk on muslin already embroidered with white sprigs of flowers. Note the subtle colours, the strange band joining the two halves and the elaborate fringes, all very typical. 19th century

be, extremely cheerful and attractive, even when the colours themselves are sombre. The background material varies. Generally it is a strong not very transparent muslin, often embroidered with sprigs of flowers. I have seen some pieces which were definitely Indian. Very occasionally this level of embroidery is coloured, usually red. The curtains may also be embroidered on plain cotton, cotton with a regular pattern such as dots – this is rare – or on net. These last are particularly fine. It is also true that in keeping with their general indifference to background material, Rabat embroideresses sometimes put months of work into a pair of curtains made of the commonest material pieced together by machine. I have seen the same phenomenon in dresses from Syria and Jordan, and Afghanistan. Although in the last case the explanation is most probably poverty, it is definitely not so with the others.

The embroidery on the curtains normally forms a solid or largely solid band at the bottom, with a *tala* or minaret-shaped design rising where the two curtains join and sometimes a little way up the outer sides as well.

Details from Rabat marriage curtains shown opposite

The embroidery can be monochrome, in which case carmine, yellow or blue is the normal choice. The polychrome possibilities are almost infinite. Particularly prized today are those with colours like stained glass, very clear and brilliant, with carmine predominating. For some reason the curtains embroidered on net are generally of this type. Personally, I like the ones with subtle rather dark colours and often as many as thirty shades – brown/black/rose/violet/grey/mauve/plum with touches of dark green and yellow, for example. One particularly magnificent single curtain, originally one of a pair, had an enormous figure-of-eight design in shades of black/dark green/dark blue, suggesting a mallard's head, the centres of the "eights" were dark stars, within their centres "eyes" of brilliant yellow, with a black "pupil" in the middle of each. The band of embroidery was particularly deep and so solid that the "eights" could only be deduced from the way the stitches lay.

Unfortunately, I have not succeeded in finding out exactly how

these curtains were used. There are two types – ordinary pairs and what are in fact pairs, but joined down the centre with a strip of very ordinary material, generally beige, a couple of inches wide. It might seem that the curtains were intended to be cut open at some stage in the marriage ceremony as a symbolic gesture, or perhaps to reveal the bride, but across the bottom there is invariably a fine trimming (of the kind at which the Moroccans excel) usually made of macramé or bobbin lace – I have also once seen crochet – in several colours, echoing the curtain. This could not have been meant to be cut. I would be *very* grateful to anyone who could shed light on the mystery!

Occasionally one comes across completely anomalous curtains. For example, I saw a pair in Tangiers which had the lower border cut from a Manila shawl and edged heavily in black. The body of the curtains was scattered with irregular oval patches cut, I think, from more than one shawl (presumably damaged) and again surrounded with black ribbon. The ground was the usual white muslin, in this case Indian. Black and carmine ribbons decorated the inner edge of the curtains and the trimming at the bottom was again black and carmine with touches of other colours. The effect was most striking, but exotic and bizarre.

The strangest pair of all, however, I bought at Rabat. They are embroidered in the style I have rather arbitrarily called Modern Rabat (see the next section) and are the only examples I know of deliberately naturalistic Rabat embroidery with human figures. The colours are sugary pastels with touches of black. The design is worked on a border along the bottom of the curtains and up the narrow band between them, which is usually made of very ordinary beige stuff. The curtains themselves are of an odd flimsy white material with a raised velvet pattern. The theme too is curious for marriage curtains – Eve (in a sort of bathing dress in the style of the 1920s) and the snake figure prominantly, there is also a large hand holding a rose, a dog which attacks the snake, one man in late 16th- or early 17th-century costume and another sitting playing a lute – a figure to be found in Greek Islands embroidery. The effect is very pretty. No-one has been able to tell me what they are, except that they were bought from a family who lived near where they were being sold in Rue des Consuls, the old foreign quarter of the city. I have a private fantasy that some Greek consul or merchant was marrying his daughter in Rabat and, liking the local custom which by then had fallen out of use in Greece, gave the embroideress patterns and symbols which meant something to him – perhaps even, in the case of the man with the lute, an old embroidered cloth. But this is the purest speculation.

Very unusual pair of marriage curtains (photograph opposite). Rabat, late 19th or early 20th century

I saw a young man cutting veil lengths of brocaded silk.
"Cut me a piece my size", I said to him.
"After you have visited me at my house", he replied,
"I will have you made a crown of gold and more besides."
"But our neighbours watch", I answered.
And he said: "They will sleep".
"I fear for my honour", was my last reply.

*   *   *

Miscellaneous pieces

Besides curtains, new Rabat embroideries include cushions, often of a very elegant long thin shape, sometimes especially designed, sometimes clearly reusing damaged curtains. As Rabat embroidery is much more delicate than, say, that of Fez — the soft floss silk tends to wear out and the relatively long stitches catch — it is quite hard to find them in good condition. Bed covers and valances were also made and what are called, rightly or wrongly, covers for dower chests, occasionally embroidered in an odd way on velvet from which the pile has been shaved; and various pieces of women's clothing. *Mendil*, or squares with all sorts of uses are quite common, as are *mherma* or handkerchiefs, and *derra* — rectangular scarves worn over the shoulders. There are also the long narrow sashes, decorated only at the ends, which served as draw-strings for the women's trousers. These last are often particularly attractive pieces — perhaps women made them for themselves and so took extra pains — and, like those from Tetouan, often reproduce the curtain designs, or part of them, in miniature.

Woman's scarf, perhaps a derra, on fine muslin, from Rabat, late 19th or early 20th century

This kind of Rabat embroidery does not seem to be done at all today. It is a great pity. I suspect that the problem is that although it is technically less demanding and certainly less time-consuming than the usual Fez-type, it cannot be taught mechanically. To draw the pattern and choose the colours requires a touch of inspiration, and once such a tradition has lapsed, it is hard to revive, although it would be well worth doing.

Modern Rabat embroidery

The embroidery which I have called "Modern Rabat" is not necessarily very modern and I am not even quite certain that it

A chest cover, Rabat, 20th century (one of a pair). Note the embroidery over shaved velvet, the curious colour scheme and the elaborate border

originated in Rabat – some say that in fact it comes from Salé – and so far no-one has been able to tell me with any authority. This type of work has something in common with the shawls of Tétouan. The older pieces are done by hand, but a great deal is being made today by machine – and has been for some time. The ground is almost invariably white and a slightly shiny effect, whether silk or synthetic, is preferred. The colour range is generally pastel, although some of the older pieces have rather stronger gradations of pink/mauve/violet/brown. There is also a type with an odd (for Morocco) colour combination of dark brown and shades of pale green. The more usual sugared almond pastels, in Tunisia at least, are considered Turkish and are particularly associated with the later painted wood-work and tiles. I have also seen pieces of embroidery, perhaps from the Greek islands rather than Turkey, with the same range of pale pink/pale blue/yellow, sometimes with touches of ivory and almond green. The pink/mauve/aubergine range suggests more the Balkans or Yugoslavia, but this again is speculation. The patterns are almost invariably floral – petalled flowers seen from above and sprays of leaves, all, as usual, very formalized.

A tkek or sash for keeping up a woman's trousers. Rabat late 19th or early 20th centuries. Note the touches of violent pink imported dye, upsetting the harmony visible in the cushion cover, p.50, and the marriage curtains, p.54.

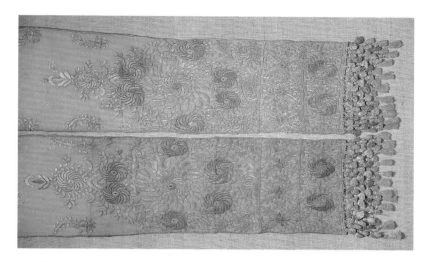

A tkek *or sash belonging to a young girl judging by the length. While the pink was once brighter than it now appears, it could never have been as harsh as that in the sash opposite. Rabat, mid-19th century*

There are, as always, occasional aberrant pieces. In *Maroc Costumes* there is illustrated a very pretty example of this type of embroidery, captioned as Salé. It is apparently one of the square chemises described under Meknès. The embroidery is basically golden yellow, with touches of pink, mauve, blue, cream, red and brown. The curious thing, however, is the design, which is suggestive of some of the Tunisian wedding tunics. A pyramid of the usual flowers and leaves rises from the two bottom corners with, facing each other in the middle, a pair of cream-coloured peacocks (really looking more like chickens) with lavender tails. They are standing on the bottom border and each has, immediately behind it, a small

Scalloped border to hang over a door or along one of the painted shelves which form an important part of North African furnishings. The stylization of the bird and grapes show French influence and the pastel colours are a taste which began early this century and are perpetuated in much machine embroidery (see also the Tétouan shawls). Rabat, early 20th century

striped brown fish, with a spray of leaves in its mouth, balanced on its tail. Higher up in the pyramid are two blue birds and two cream ones, these last enclosed in red coronets and one of them so stylized as to be unrecognizable. There are similar birds round the neck. On either side of the pyramid swims a yellow fish with a rose inside its body. The effect is attractive but odd. The symbolism of both fish and birds is discussed at greater length in the section on Tunisia (see pp. 110, 112-3). Another comparable piece bought at Rabat is a fragment of a border, judging by the scalloping, and the design represents pairs of birds facing each other across bunches of grapes, worked in mauve and pale yellow on white.

The pieces found or made today – I believe they all date from this century – are as a rule connected with women's dress: handkerchiefs, scarves, sashes, veils (sometimes worked very fetchingly on completely transparent chiffon), robes and caftans. This type of embroidery does not seem to be done on bed- or other household linen, although it would undoubtedly have greater appeal to the European eye than the darker and heavier Fez-work, especially for hand-towels and sheets. It is in any case very rarely sold in "tourist shops", although it can easily be found at any of the numerous small workshops in the back streets of the Medina of any major town. For some reason this machine embroidery and Fez hand embroidery have become the two standard styles all over Morocco today.

SALÉ

Salé is the twin town of Rabat, standing opposite it at the mouth of the Bou Regreg – Ptolemy's River Sala – where the river flows into the Atlantic. In Roman times it seems to have been known as Salacolonia, although there are no very visible remains there today. The date of the founding of present-day Salé is imprecise – somewhere between the 8th and 11th centuries – and its history has been extremely turbulent. Among other attackers, occasionally successful, were the Spaniards, and as a result of the Reconquista various waves of refugees from Andalusia settled at Salé. Those of 1609-1610 came predominantly from San Lucar and Cadiz. Salé was also a very active trading port throughout the Middle Ages and merchants from England and Flanders came to buy, among other things, wool, cloth and carpets. The Genoese, Pisans, Venetians and Catalans, on the other hand, went there to sell their velvets, brocades and manufactured goods. Later, Salé became famous above all for its corsairs, recruited quite largely from European renegades. This gave the city a new and rather different cosmopolitan atmosphere.

The Embroidery

Salé produced large quantities of embroidery, which has points of similarity with the work from Fez, Meknès and Chéchaouen, but curiously enough is quite different from that of Rabat, a quarter of a mile away across the river. Rabat embroidery designs are generally drawn freehand, while Salé embroidery is all counted thread work. Another oddity of Salé is that while the curtains were worked on the Turkish style wooden frame as at Fez, for the other pieces the tightly stuffed Andalusian pillow was used as at Rabat.

Old Salé embroidery

There are two main styles of Salé embroidery. That known as "Old Salé", although individual examples are not necessarily very antique and mostly seem to date back to the 19th century, which is done in the kind of bouclé effect we have already seen in zone (b) of the Chéchaouen embroideries. This is often used for

Salé cushion end show-ing right side (dark) and wrong side (light). This piece has a minimal amount of pattern pro-vided by leaving very small areas of the back-ground uncovered, which is unusual. Salé, 19th cen-tury

Much simplified border of a Salé curtain, the black (in fact indigo) is elabor-ately diapered, the white represents the back-ground cloth left blank.

monochrome cushion ends on which the embroidery is so dense that it is impossible to see any trace of pattern and even the blocks of stitches or *bait* are only noticeable as the light falls on them. These cushions — curtain borders also seem occasionally to have been done this way — are invariably a deep carmine or a very dark blue. They are worked in silk on a rather closely woven white cotton or linen and, being very durable, are commonly found.

Sometimes the design on these monochrome cushions is still identifiable — and probably at the earliest date would always have been. There is, for example, the pattern called *ras el-arusa* or "Head of the Bride", in which the elements which we would think of as a vase flanked by cypress trees are seen as a girl's face between two braids of hair, and the various leaves and branches are consi-dered to be the heavy hair ornaments and strings of emeralds and baroque pearls which are traditional elements in the bridal dress and held to bring good luck.

There are also polychrome pieces worked in bouclé, the finest of which date to the late 18th and early 19th centuries and include both cushions (but these may be reused pieces) and curtain

Salé cushion end, 19th century. Note "Hand of Fatima", top left

borders. The Salé bouclé stitch is particularly suitable for the latter being reversible. The curtains were typically made in three vertical strips, the embroidered part forming a lower border 30-60 cm high. The strips were subsequently sewn together and a minaret-shaped embroidered decoration called *tala*, rising 50 cm or more above the main border, was worked to embellish the seam.

One beautiful early example in a private collection has a very elaborate border beginning with a row of stylized trees, alternating with trees with storks, as those at Fez, with below a line of eight-pointed flowers, in which every other one is shown in negative by leaving the petals white. The line of flowers is enclosed by embroidered "ribbons". All this is basically worked in old rose, with touches of other colours – ivory, moss green and old gold for the centres of the flowers. Next comes a "ribbon" of soft deep greyish blue, followed by a broad band of very fine drawn-thread work in white, another geometric ribbon, this time in old rose, and finally another deep frieze of two different types of stylized trees in the grey blue. Effects such as this – much subtler and less mechanical than in Fez embroidery – are fairly standard in the oldest pieces, which are, alas, rare and often fragmentary. The alternating full and empty eight-petalled flowers are particularly characteristic and attractive.

Detail of an unusually fine Salé bedcover or hanging. Note the alternating tree and stork in a tree pattern along the top edge, the eight-petalled flowers characteristic of Salé and the "river" of a needle-weaving across the centre. Salé, late 18th or early 19th century

Modern Salé embroidery

The so-called "Modern Salé" embroidery is non-reversible and is used particularly for cushions. It is worked largely in back stitch and darning stitches with touches of cross stitch – actually, many of the motifs can be adapted to cross stitch with a very pleasant effect. The colours of these polychrome pieces are strong, but attractive. A deep carmine tends to predominate (as in all Salé work) and often, where the motifs follow each other in different colours, there will be one red element for every – say – yellow, blue or green.

Quite often the designs are almost entirely geometric, with friezes of "minarets" and bands of figures such as elongated hexagons (a particularly favourite motif), hexagons containing stars or four-petalled "flowers", lozenges, squares, diamonds, and so on. These borders are generally edged with embroidered "ribbons", commonly of a darker colour with small paler crosses. Another favourite motif is a spray of leaves or flowers worked diagonally in a square and so formalized as to have become virtually abstract. Possible colour combinations include the common carmine/sea green/yellow/deep blue type mentioned above, or sometimes paler effects such as a dominant soft carmine with rose/pale violet/grey-mauve/brownish-black, or, again, dominant soft carmine and two shades of yellow-ivory with touches of violet/natural/light and dark brown/coral. This last is much rarer.

Fragment of a Salé border, probably from a cushion. Both pattern and colours are typical, but the pale yellow would have probably been green before fading. First half of the 19th century

The friezes of "minarets", as Mme Guérard points out in her exhaustive study, are really extremely stylized trees and flowers. She has also suggested that some of the patterns represent lamps — a very ancient Christian and pre-Christian symbol and one much used in Islam, particularly on prayer rugs, no doubt on account of the famous verses of the Koran from the Surah of Light:

> "God is the light of the heavens and the earth. His light is like a lamp set in a niche, a lamp within a crystal like a star."

Words which have so often been the subject of calligraphy — on paper, stone, tile, carpets, and also in embroidery.

The locals, incidentally, now call these lamp-shapes *tyour* — birds.

The analogies should not be pushed too far, but it is interesting to consider certain similarities between the embroideries of Salé and those of the Greek Islands. These stylized sprays of flowers, so common in Turkish and Greek embroidery, become, especially in Greece, as Pauline Johnstone points out, completely formal and worked into a square with the stem as the diagonal, bordered by a row of similar bunches placed side by side, all the stems being at the same angle. This, as we have seen, is a favourite motif at Salé.

Embroideries from Rhodes are worked, like those from Old Salé, in a very loosely twisted floss silk, which curls to produce Rhodian or Astrakhan Stitch, in which it is difficult to see the individual stitches. Here, cross stitch may be used, often worked haphazard, as sometimes seen at Salé, or it can be worked in step stitch, again a Moroccan favourite.

A typical Rhodian colour combination is brick red and green. There is a vague similarity to some of the work from Karpathos. A dress now in the Victorian and Albert Museum, London, described in the marriage settlement as a "best dress", also has an air of North Africa with its red-green-red-blue alternation, so popular at Salé.

It might also be interesting to compare some of the geometric elements with those described by A.J.B. Wace for the Cyclades and the Dodecanese. The pattern which he calls the King Pattern — a stem with pairs of conventional leaves, another version of the Tree of Life — appears also in the embroideries of Fez and Meknès, and even of Rabat. A version of the more elaborate Queen Pattern (these motifs of course have all kinds of local names among the islands), occasionally appears alternating with the tree in Salé and Fez borders. The third basic floral pattern, the vase of flowers or *glastra* (Rhodes), yet another development of the Tree of Life, is common in North Africa, generally in a very stylized form and, much more realistically represented, is a great favourite in Turkey.

It should not, of course, be forgotten that in the 17th century there were a number of Greeks at Salé — the islands were poor, piracy was lucrative and, like the North Europeans, they had a fine reputation as seamen and were much in demand.

Samplers

Samplers made by the girls at the end of their apprenticeship to the *ma'allema* survive from many of the towns in Morocco and are particularly charming pieces. They are also interesting since they show the range of motifs in common use and, being polychrome, they give some hint of the colour sense of their day. For some reason they are relatively common from Salé, which may be chance, or may indicate something about the local teaching arrangements. There is a particularly nice sampler, or *telleqa*, in the Musée des Arts Africains et Océaniens in Paris. It dates from the late 18th century, but it is not certain where in North Morocco it was

made, as the 12 or 13 different borders and 6 panels show a mixture of motifs. The sampler has some silver work and is nicely edged with tassels. It also includes a couple of lines of calligraphy — very rare in North African non-gold embroidery, presumably because the women were illiterate — carefully worked and vowelled, but unfortunately almost indecipherable (perhaps "With power and restraint one attains high things", or possibly more likely, "With modesty and silence one attains wisdom").

An exceptionally fine sampler unfortunately somewhat faded, showing numerous stitches and motifs from Algeria or north Morocco, late 18th century

Ma'allema

P. Ricard in 1918 wrote: "It was hard enough for me to get in touch with embroideresses in Rabat, but it was completely impossible in Salé."

This has entirely changed, partly no doubt as a result of the gradual emancipation of women, who now own their own shops and deal directly with the public (an almost entirely female public, of course), and partly thanks to the French efforts to revive local crafts which, although they involved some breaking up of strictly regional traditions, had the immense merit of saving many crafts from vanishing absolutely.

Salé today has a large number of embroidery workshops. Typically placed in small back streets of the medina, they consist of a window displaying one or two pieces of work, curtained so that passers-by cannot see through. The door is similarly "veiled". Inside there is a tiny shop with very little work actually for sale, since most of it is commissioned. As a rule there is, over most of the shop, an upstairs balcony where two or three girls and the older *ma'alle-ma* work, either at hand-done Fez embroidery or at the new-style machine embroidery of Rabat. None of them do Salé embroidery in the normal course of events. One particularly elderly *ma'allema* with a shop just off the *kissaria* thought it might be feasible to copy a piece, given time and if it were "not too difficult". The whole idea was received with a distinct lack of enthusiasm.

Unfortunately it was not possible, as I had hoped, to meet Mme Alaoui, the local expert on – significantly enough – Fez embroidery and the author of several pattern books, who might well have been able to enlighten me as to the real state of Salé work today.

TÉTOUAN

Tétouan is a medium-sized town, very beautifully sited in a valley looking out over the mountains of the Rif, and close to the classical site of Tamuda, which dates from the 2nd or 3rd century BC. Tétouan itself was founded in 1306 or 1307 and was very prosperous until it was sacked by Henry III of Castille, who killed half the people and deported the rest to Spain. The town remained deserted for a century, but was repopulated after the fall of Granada by Muslim and Jewish refugees; further waves arrived at intervals, particularly as a result of the expulsion of the "Moors" by Philip III in the early 17th century. Tétouan continued to have a rather uneven relationship with Spain until 1956.

The Embroidery

From the point of view of the visitor, Tétouan is not a particularly lively town for embroidery today – although, judging by the quantity of shops selling thread, a good deal must be done domestically. There are a number of *ma'allema*, however, producing the fairly standard Fez and Rabat-style work discussed elsewhere; and of course the usual jellabas. There is also a very handsome local style of these, often handwoven in elaborate patterns in natural shades of wool, or sometimes plain brown with bold embroideries in heavy thread. These are to be seen on the people from the hills, but are not easily bought – I have tried. Since this is a heavily Berber area, it is not surprising that the weaving is more satisfactory than the embroidery at a market level: pleasant blankets and rugs are made on the spot for local use and there are also the very gay red and white striped cloths worn by the women of the Rif.

The traditional embroideries of Tétouan are very distinctive and quite unlike anything else in Morocco. It has been suggested, very convincingly, that their origin, their distant origin at least, is Turkish and this is born out by the designs, choice of colours and stitches. This is curious since Tétouan's links were, as we have seen, much more obviously with Spain than with the Levant. There were, however, also connections with Algeria and Algerian refugees came to Tétouan last century, which meant that the Turkish influence may have arrived at one remove, since Algiers itself was under Turkish domination for centuries. The local embroideresses traditionally did not, however, use the Turkish embroidery frame, but pinned the cloth on a tightly stuffed cushion folded in two and held on their knees in the Spanish manner. The finished parts of the embroidery are carefully wrapped in a clean cloth for protection.

A. Joly, writing on industry in Tétouan in 1909, mentions that out of a population of some 25,000 Muslims, roughly 1,000 of the women embroidered at home, adding that this was a lower proportion than at Fez. He also says that for embroidering an 'ajar or hanging, the woman would be paid 17-23 basitas per month and that the work would take her 45-60 days. Allowing 35 basitas for the raw materials and something for extras, this brought the price of a hanging to about 100 basitas. It is very hard to calculate the value of money in the past in real terms, but it has been suggested that this would have had a buying power in the order of £50-£100. Today (1983) it would cost around £40-£150 to buy an old one, but no-one could begin to quote for having a new one made.

A. Joly adds that the patterns were drawn onto the cloth by the ma'allemat, who were of course paid for this, and that this outline was known as rechem. He also mentions that some of the wealthy folk of Tétouan liked curtains and hangings of silk and velvet embroidered with gold and silver (compare the Chéchaouen stars) and that the Jewish women wore velvet dresses of great splendour decorated in this way. There was a sizeable mellah, or Jewish quarter, at Tétouan and it is not unlikely that they were responsible for most or all of this kind of work.

Tétouan is the only city in Morocco to use precious materials as a ground for embroidery, other than gold embroidery. The earliest pieces – late 18th or early 19th century – are worked on a very fine strong white or natural linen, occasionally as light as muslin (originally, incidentally, from Mosul) and reminiscent of that used for some of the 18th-century Turkish towels. The later pieces, including those made earlier this century, are on silk or satin. This silk is of a taffeta (from the Persian "to be lustrous") type, which tends to split and tear round the edge of the embroidery. The satin is much more solid. The colours used are pink, pale blue, scarlet and yellow, the last being much the most common, and very occasionally, dark green.

The colours of the embroidery depend on the ground, but are always very brilliant: red/white/navy/royal blue/pale turquoise, with a little green, and black outlines for the red white and green, on a yellow satin background; or white/yellow/mid-blue/blue-violet, with touches of turquoise and green, and again black outlines, on pink. The colour schemes of the earlier pieces on natural linen tend to be somewhat different and, predictably, more subtle. There is a

Tensifa – or mirror veil – worked on fine linen, late 18th century Tétouan. Note the design and colour of the early pieces, and the elegant borders, Tensifas always have a more elaborate edge on the right than the left; I do not know why this is

particularly fine example in the Fitzwilliam Museum, Cambridge – a mirror veil, with beautifully designed and worked borders, and the colours are essentially lemon/purple/peach/white/various shades of bright pale blue/palish grass green/light carmine/peacock.

The thread used is quite a fine silk and the stitches are mostly variants of brick stitch – for example the one known as Algerian filling stitch – sometimes leaving out alternate "bricks" to show the cloth, but more often entirely covering the ground. A kind of couching is sometimes used – long threads being laid down and then caught with smaller stitches, but there is always a definite tendency towards the brick arrangement ‾–‾–‾ . The outlines – for each block of lighter colour is defined by a dark outline – are stem stitch or black stitch.

*   *   *

Cheeks like roses sprinkled in the morning with pearls
of dew
For you I long to have a room bright with splendid
hangings richly worked
Where I may pass my nights in adoration and thus slake
my fires.
There is nothing above the love you inspire in me
but God Most High.

Ajar or horizontal wall-hanging-Tétouan second half of the 19th century. This colour scheme was by far the most popular at the period. Yellow taffeta is sometimes used instead of satin

The range of objects made is comparatively limited. Firstly there are the hangings – 'ajar – strips around 1 m deep and 2-3 m long (although they vary greatly) intended to be hung horizontally, decorating the bed alcove for marriages, and no doubt circumcisions and other great occasions, and comparable to the hangings from Chéchaouen and elsewhere. They are generally embroidered with a border along their length and then scattered floral compositions, very faintly reminiscent in arrangement of paisley "cones", over the body of the piece.

There are also the uniquely Tétouan pieces known as *tensifa*, or mirror veils. They are about 50 cm wide and can be as much as 3.50 m to 5.50 m long. They were used, it is said, to hide the long mirrors in the house for the duration of the honeymoon, which in that part of Morocco is considered to last forty days. The loveliest and oldest ones are embroidered on muslin in soft colours, but the basic design remains very constant from first to last. A piece, already mentioned, in the Fitzwilliam Museum, Cambridge is typical and the following diagram will serve to show the lay-out of the *tensifa* in its most elaborate form:

Flying flower or butterfly from a Tétouan tensifa.

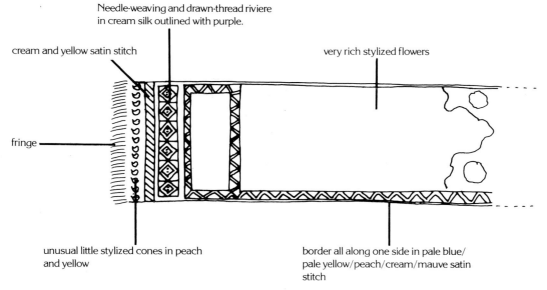

Needle-weaving and drawn-thread riviere in cream silk outlined with purple.

cream and yellow satin stitch

very rich stylized flowers

fringe

unusual little stylized cones in peach and yellow

border all along one side in pale blue/pale yellow/peach/cream/mauve satin stitch

Tétouan Figure 1

In this particular case, there is no sign that the pattern was drawn on the cloth and it may have been worked freehand, as were most Turkish embroideries, for example, and as Rajastani embroideries often are even today.

Tétouan embroidery was also used for cushions, which were sometimes, as elsewhere, made up at a later date out of damaged larger pieces. The embroideries intended for use as cushions are generally on a white or natural cotton ground and have first a narrow band of stylized flowers enclosed by an embroidered line above and below to form a "ribbon", with above it a wide frieze, again of stylized flowers often arranged at a slant. Cushions are rare, perhaps because the stitches used, unlike those at Fez, cause the work to wear out easily and therefore few have survived. There are also fragments of square pieces which may have been *mendil*.

*   *   *

Embroideress, embroideress,
Embroider me a sash
To give to Tahra,
When she returns from Our Lady
                              Mecca.

*   *   *

Tétouan embroidery was apparently not much used for clothing. The only items regularly found are *tkek*, the sashes which serve as draw-strings for women's baggy trousers. These are quite common, generally of satin, and naturally only embroidered at the ends with an arrangement not unlike that of the *tensifa*, but in miniature. It is said that women's veils were also embroidered, but unfortunately I have never seen one.

The elements which make up a piece of Tétouan embroidery are essentially stylized flowers. Mme Guérard has written most interestingly of their evolution and takes her argument back to a very fine velvet prayer carpet from Bursa in Turkey, dating to the late 16th century, which shows a number of flowers represented in a way very similar to those at Tétouan.

The tulip, omnipresent in Turkish art, is rather surprisingly missing (although at least two kinds of wild tulip grow in abundance over North Africa), but the carnation is there, very stylized, the wild rose, the hyacinth — so reduced that it often looks more like a butterfly, or else with its bells ending in tendrils like question marks — and the strange horseshoe-shaped figure which is in all likelihood a pomegranate. The pomegranate is, for obvious reasons, a fertility symbol in almost every country where it is known, from China to the classical world — the six seeds so fatally eaten by Persephone on her descent to the underworld will be remembered. In Islam, it is a common motif in art and poetry, and perhaps it should not be forgotten that Aisha, the favourite wife of Muhammad, whose name means "The Living One", was the daughter of Umm Rumman, "The Mother of the Pomegranate". Pomegran-

Bunch of flowers –
Tétouan.

Tensifa – or mirror veil – Tétouan late 19th century. Compare with the one on p.73 for change in taste over that century

ates stylized very similarly to those of Tétouan appear in Balkan embroideries and on Turkish towels. It is said, on what ultimate authority I do not know, that when a young Turkish bride found herself with child for the first time, she would often embroider a cloth with fruit, generally pomegranates, and send it to her mother-in-law, rather than explain her condition face-to-face. Personally, I have never met a woman in the Middle East who was shy about such things, but presumably it is possible. Surprisingly, the water-melon which is a similar symbol, on account of its numerous seeds, from China to Turkey never to my knowledge appears in North African embroidery, although melons are widely eaten.

The Tétouan compositions, especially on the ends of *tensifa* or sashes, tend to alternate flowers and pomegranates in slanting lines, building up a pile with an elaborate "cone" on top. The spaces are filled with sprays of leaves – sprigs of the Tree of Life, perhaps? – and the abbreviated hyacinths which look like butterflies.

A number of the Tétouan patterns had traditional names: one of the scattered, vaguely floral, motifs was known as *settaba* – broom, and another as *besmaq* – wooden shoes. As in so many areas around the Mediterranean, notably the Greek islands and Palestine, the names of the motifs seem to have nothing to do with the actual patterns and are sometimes quite perversely switched: star for moon and moon for star in a Syrian village, for example. A study of the Tétouan names has been made by P. Ricard.

Gold embroidery from Tétouan

The Jewish women of Tétouan were famous for their embroidery and it is probable that they produced much or all of the gold embroidery of the type presented by the Chéchaouen appliqué stars.

There is, unfortunately, insufficent space to discuss costume, but a mention should be made of the marriage costume of the Jewish women. In spite of certain restrictions and sumptuary laws, the Jewish women of North Africa were famous for the splendour of their dress, those of the island of Djerba, for example, often being walking advertisements for their husbands' merchandise, for the Jews there were largely connected with the cloth industry and trade.

In Morocco, although Jewish women usually veiled – drawing their *haik* across half their face and leaving one eye exposed to differentiate them from Muslims – they were nevertheless freer than the Arab women and their clothes were consequently more accurately known to Europeans. The most striking costume of the Jewish women was the *kiswa el-kabira* which was given to the bride, as part of her dowry, by her father and was subsequently worn for feast days, weddings and circumcisions. The principal embroidered pieces were the bolero or *gonbaiz*, with its splendid buttons, the *hezam* or wide velvet belt richly embroidered with gold, and the *jelteta*, a kind of wrap-over skirt typically of claret, dark green or black velvet, ankle length and with a most magnificent "sun-burst" of gold embroidery radiating up from the bottom corner almost to the waist. The fashion is said to date back to 16th-century Spain. The Tangier version is the most famous, partly on account of Delacroix's watercolour of a Jewish bride whose wedding he attended in 1832. There is also a good drawing done by Victor

Eeckhout in 1878. For the rest, this costume has been admirably described and illustrated in Alfred Rubens' work.

The women of Tétouan were considered to make the finest *kiswa el-kabira* and examples of their (and other regions') workmanship are still sometimes offered for sale.

Kettafiya

The small rectangular pieces known as *kettafiya*, or shoulder cloths, are mentioned by Mme Guérard, who says that when she was in Tétouan she was told that they were used by young girls on their marriage day to cover their shoulders during the hair-dressing before the marriage. Like applying henna to the hands and feet, this is a ritual occasion. These rare pieces, embroidered with much very fine gold and, more recently, a little coloured silk, on a ground of natural or white silk or cotton, often brocaded, are charming. The occasional stylized flowers, especially along the borders, are reminiscent of the main school of Tétouan embroidery, but the gold scrolls and curlicues are much more similar to the *bniqa*, or hair coverings, from Algiers, or even some of the 18th-century towels or scarves from Turkey. Pieces with the same name, finely woven but typically not embroidered, are worn on the shoulders as part of formal dress in Médenine and Tozeur in Southern Tunisia.

Shawls

> *My silken scarf,*
> *Scarf bought with its weight in gold,*
> *You shall tie it on your head,*
> *Oh my Zahra, to me so dear!*

*   *   *

Although this book is not much concerned with machine embroidery, there is one last curiosity from Tétouan which strikes me as worthy of mention. In Tétouan, and elsewhere in North Morocco, very pleasant shawls are offered for sale which are vaguely reminiscent of the Manila or Canton shawls so popular in Spain. They have long fringes and are almost invariably machine-embroidered with flowers — stylized chrysanthemums and peonies being the most common – which clearly originate from China, but are arranged in a typically Tétouan manner, alternating tidily in diagonal rows. The colour combinations are three: white on white; very delicate pastels – sugared-almond colours – on white; slightly stronger colours on a pastel ground. The long fringes are white on the white shawls, but on the others they are of two colours, two adjacent sides being, say, pink or primrose, and the other two lavender or pale green.

I was told by one dealer – but I do not know whether it is correct – that the local people much admired the Spanish women's shawls earlier this century (the Spaniards occupied Tétouan from 1913-1956) but could not afford them and so imitated them as best they could. Apparently it became the fashion to wear them not round the shoulders but round the hips and later as head coverings – all white for the Jews, pastel on white for the Muslims, and a coloured ground for the Christians: fascinating information, if true. Certainly Manila and Spanish imitation-Manila shawls are quite often to be found in North Morocco, generally in very poor condition.

LACE

All over North Africa, but particularly in Morocco, a wide range of extremely nice trimmings – fringes, borders, needleworked and plaited buttons, braids, tassels, cords, and so on are made. Oddly enough it is usually a male occupation and it is very common to see young men in Rabat or Fez working at the doors of their shops, while their younger brothers turn the whole streets into a cats' cradle as they twist together the skeins of silk thread. In the past year or two, small electric motors detached from egg-beaters and such like have come into use.

It is not possible, unfortunately, to discuss all these trimmings here, although those made of metal thread are exhaustively and technically described by M. Goichon; but, since so few people are aware of its existence, I would like to say a few words about North African lace.

Needle lace

Tunisia, Algeria and Morocco all produced needle lace and a large number of designs and very good descriptions can be found in the works of P. Comte and P. Ricard. It is hard to tell when this kind of lace began to be made in the area, but quite possibly before the coming of the French, although probably not, as occasionally suggested, as far back as the 17th century, brought by refugees from Andalusia. It cannot be stated too strongly that this is an area which has been open to the most varied cultural influences and it is almost impossible, since there are no records, to establish which particular wind blew a given technique there. It has, however, been put forward by P. Ricard that since this kind of lace-making is largely associated with the Turkish possessions in North Africa, and especially with Algiers, once Khairadin and Barbarossa's first capital, that Algerian lace at least is of Eastern rather than European origin. This view is supported by very similar lace from the Syria-Jordan area and from Asia Minor.

All sorts of things were made out of this lace, including – the list is from Algeria – inserts for the fronts and seams of women's caftans and trousers (seams typically are treated as decorative in

North Africa and are enriched with ribbons, gold embroidery, and so on – for example, the *tala* on Rabat and Salé curtains), collars, scarves, fichus, handkerchiefs, squares for covering trays, cloths for covering men's turbans, and also their weapons at night, inserts for pillows and bed covers and the decorative strips used to join the two lengths of cloth making up the *mlaya* (pl. *mlayat*) or veil of the type worn by the black women – somewhat different styles of dress were favoured by different ethnic groups; the ordinary *chadur* of Iran is made in the same way, but without the lace.

Especially in Tunisia, lace is much used for the wide bell-shaped sleeves, which were – and still are – an important part of the traditional dress worn on special occasions. These sleeves can measure a metre or more at the wrist and their whiteness and transparency contrasts pleasantly with the often very heavy and brilliant gold and silk embroidery of the main costume. They are generally made in such a way as to be detachable and the chemise of which they are part is mostly of ordinary cotton edged with broderie anglaise.

This kind of lace is worked on a small cushion and is not very complicated, although requiring good eyesight and endless patience. The pattern is made by leaving gaps in the basic network of stitches and these are given endearing names, which vary from town to town: at Algiers – a row of little cakes, honeycomb, full chequer board, empty chequer board, and so on. The basic net made of large hexagons is called *khatem Sidna Sliman* – seal of our Lord Solomon, because it looks like a six-pointed star. The seal of Solomon is a powerful and frequently recurring symbol in both Islamic art and folklore. Our Solomon Seal (*polygonatum multi-florum*), incidentally, takes its name from the similar pattern made by a section of the root or by the point of attachment of the stem, and it was believed to be very efficacious for "sealing" wounds. At Tunis, zigzags are called arches, a square of large open links – apples, slanted lines of large open links – sabres, while any brick-type pattern is *zellij* – tiles.

In North Africa, it is very hard to establish names for anything, even within one town, and it may be fairly assumed there will be a local name for practically everything. This kind of lace is called *tesrif* in Tunis, *driboz* in Algeria and another commonly-used word especially for the inserts is *chebka*, commemorated on a recent issue of 75 millime Tunisian stamps by a picture of a girl making lace on a cushion. Again, at Rabat the word is *randa* – conceivably from the town of Ronda in Spain? One could go on and on.

Needle lace is sometimes made in silk or of thread composed of gold or silver over a silk core, for narrow borders, never large pieces, and apparently very occasionally calligraphic patterns are to be found, although I personally have never seen one.

Moroccan needle lace differs slightly from Algerian and Tunisian in that a thicker thread and smaller, tighter links produce a denser effect.

This kind of lace is still made in various parts of North Africa, although it no longer enjoys the vogue for trimming clothes that it did in the 1920s and 1930s, but is used more for mats, tray-cloths and such like – in Tunis it is even possible to buy lace good-luck fish!

Algerian and Tunisian embroidery on tulle

P. Ricard describes in his book on lace the very attractive "veils" of hand-embroidered tulle worn by the little girls in one of the villages near Tlemcen. This kind of work done on machine-made tulle (6-7 links per cm) with an ordinary embroidery needle and white thread, sometimes, but not necessarily, on an embroidery frame was, and perhaps still is, a speciality of the Oran-Tlemcen region. The effect is pretty and relatively quick to do. No-one seems to know where the idea came from or when it originated, although it is presumably quite recent. Conceivably it may have begun with copying the white on white muslin North Indian embroideries which were imported into North Africa last century.

One striking thing about these embroideries, according to P. Ricard, is the care with which the fairly numerous motifs are identified and named: keys, bushes, dried raisins, spare ribs, melon seeds, half an eggplant, half an eggplant and fritters on a plate, candelabra with candles, teapot, butterfly, bowl of couscous with milk, folded velvet, pigeons' feet, and little hunchback with a cake, to name but a few.

To our eyes, none of them – mostly spots, rings, squares, flowers, sprigs and stars – have anything at all to do with their names, but this is fairly normal around the Mediterranean, as has been mentioned before.

In Tunisia a technically similar type of work is to be found on the sleeves of the famous Raf-Raf marriage tunics. Here, coloured thread, almost invariably wool, is used and the pattern is dense, not scattered, covering the whole of the sleeve, which is approximately square and measures approximately 30 cm long and 55-60 cm round. The patterns, basically geometric, are quite varied, but there are two main types of arrangement. The everyday tunics normally have an all-over pattern in colours only. The formal tunics, in particular those worn on the third day of the marriage, have more splendid sleeves with couched gold thread, canetilla (tubular beads) and sequins embroidered on over the wool. The designs, often enclosed within borders of canetilla, are most often flowers, stars, crescents, hearts, circles, leaves and, sometimes, fish. Typically there is a horizontal band round the "cuff" and the rest of the sleeve is worked in vertical strips, with a "ribbon" of rather solid gold embroidery running down the centre from the point of the shoulder over the cuff band. The underarm sector is usually embroidered much more sparingly with gold, or not at all, both because it would not be seen and to prevent the metal cutting into the embroidery on the main body of the tunic.

Raf-Raf sleeve showing wool on net embroidery.

Basically the embroidery is done by passing the wool, with an ordinary needle, through the links in the tulle, one over, one under. A square embroidery frame with feet may or may not be used. Little girls generally begin to learn this technique on a comparatively coarse tulle, making the white and coloured (sometimes pastel) sleeves of their everyday tunics, and eventually working up to their marriage robes. Lines of the type of running stitch just described are varied with chevrons, arrow-head stitch, thorn stitch, fish-bone stitch, and so on. Curvilinear stitches are not used. For some reason cross stitch is almost unknown, but a great favourite is a star formed by making the stitches radiate out from one central hole – basically Algerian eye, or star, stitch. There is a considerable range of colour schemes, but brilliant purple/blue/peacock/green/pink/magenta is a particular favourite; the colours always tend towards the bright, but are beautifully combined and are extremely gay, not garish.

I have never consciously seen a piece of Raf-Raf tulle embroidery made earlier than this century. It is still made, but those examples offered for sale, at least, are not very fine and the gold thread is tinselly and poor and the sequins plastic.

The only examples I have come across of this in Morocco are certain Rabati curtains, but there the net is treated like any other background material.

Embroidery on net

The long strips of embroidery on the heavy square link net which in Europe is called *filet*, with designs very similar to those in the embroideries of Azemmour, were at first thought to be of French origin, but it is now fairly well established that they were made earlier in Morocco and both the technique and the Renaissance designs suggest the craft is derived from the refugees from Spain in the early 17th century. A more romantic, but less well-documented, story tells how it was brought to North Africa by Spanish girls captured from the coastal towns by the rovers of Salé and sold into slavery.

Found almost exclusively at Rabat, it is not known how long this type of embroidery has been made, but the patterns – floral scrolls, S-type patterns, grotesques, for example two seahorse-like creatures on either side of a chalice or vase – are those of the Spanish or Italian 17th century. The embroidery is done on a very fine net of 5-6 holes to the centimetre in a darning stitch, but the designs do not have the clarity of their European counterparts on account of the much thicker thread used.

Serious efforts were made to revive this craft by Mme Navicet in 1916-17, with admirable results from the technical point of view, but sadly the exercise did not prove viable commercially, and died.

Azemmour crocheted lace

This again is presumably a recent introduction and one which had a very short life. The pieces made were almost always strips and used a number of the traditional Azemmour designs — doves and a vase, chimaeras, scrolls, and so on, although there are also innovations, for example a row of very peculiar-looking camels.

At Azemmour, crocheted lace seems to have been a Jewish speciality.

Bag made out of a Raf-Raf embroidery sleeve. First half of the 20th century.

Rabat bobbin lace

Locally known as *lingache*, this type of lace is again rare and had a short life — probably mid-19th to early 20th century. The only clue to its origin is that each loop is called *pnit* — clearly not Arabic or Berber, since these languages have no p, but presumably from the Italian or Spanish *punto* — stitch.

Drawn thread work

Bands, which the French call "rivers", of drawn-thread work and needle-weaving are quite common, as we have seen, in North African embroidery, especially that of Chéchaouen, but also elsewhere, as an elegant way of finishing off a border. The "river" may be whitework, coloured, or in very fine gold and silver thread. It is quite usual on Turkish towels and also in Persian embroidery. There is a full description of how to work these bands in Th. de Dillmont's *Encyclopédie des ouvrages des dames* under "jours de toile". In Morocco, they are called *mesloul*.

*   *   *

Weep for Seville like a bereaved father,
But remember the women in lace,
Their cold ornaments once
Led us to the sun-rise.

*   *   *

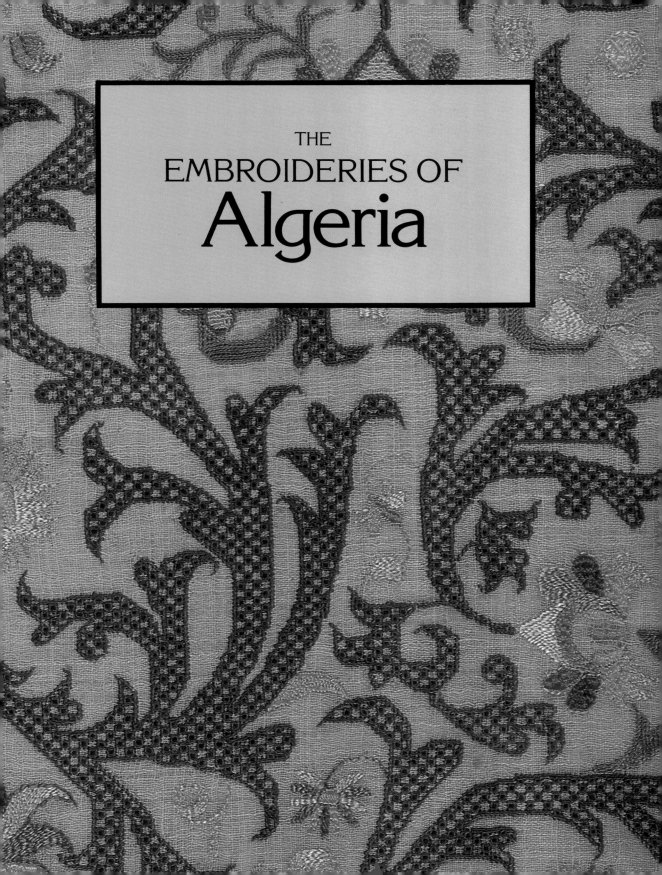

THE
EMBROIDERIES OF
Algeria

*"The fortune left by the parents may be exhausted,
But the skill of the two hands remains."*

A princess married and carried to her husband's palace a dazzling trousseau and splendid jewels. After certain reverses, her husband could no longer keep her in any reasonable style. She therefore began to sell her jewels one at a time and in the end her trousseau wore out. One day the king sent the black wet-nurse to ask for news of his daughter and the princess answered:

"That which his Majesty gave me has departed, but that which my mother gave me remains."
Annoyed, the king called his wife:
"Answer at once," he said, "what is this inexhaustible treasure with which you dowered the girl?"
"My lord," replied the mother, "I gave her nothing you did not know about — I taught her a skill."

Detail of 'Algerian sampler'

Introduction

On the whole, less is known about Algerian embroidery than Tunisian or Moroccan and, unfortunately, Algeria is a country I have had very little opportunity to visit. However, what does seem to be clear from the available collections in Algiers and elsewhere is that old Algerian embroidery is much closer to Turkish than to any of the other North African styles. As in Tunisia and Morocco, there is, in addition to silk embroidery, embroidery with metal thread on velvet or leather, essentially self-coloured embroidery much used on men's robes, and a certain amount of rustic embroidery, about which I know almost nothing, but would very much appreciate any information my readers can give me.

It is hardly surprising that Turkish influence should have been strong in Algeria. Khairaddin Barbarossa took Algiers in 1516, made it a centre for his corsair activities throughout the Mediterranean (under the protection of the Sultan at Istanbul) and extended his power over most of the coastal cities – the situation was different in the largely Berber hinterland – with the exception of Oran, which remained Spanish until 1792. In 1830, the Algerians, aided by the French, expelled the Turks, only to find the French in their place. On 10th September, 1962, the forces of Colonel Boumédienne entered Algiers – the country was, after nearly 450 years, self-governed and independent at last.

Like other countries in North Africa, Algeria was traditionally more given to weaving than embroidery, and there are magnificent pieces from Djebel Amour in the Djidjelli region north of Constantine, for example, and from elsewhere in the Berber country, and pleasant carpets are still made today.

The silk embroidery with which we are mostly concerned is clearly from the coastal cities, most notably from Algiers itself, although there were undoubtedly regional styles at Oran, perhaps with Spanish influence, Béjaïa (Bougie), Tlemcen, Constantine, Annaba (Bône) and one or two other centres.

ALGIERS

The name of Algiers in Arabic is *al-Jezāir* – the islands. These once protected the port, but have now vanished in the course of various dredging and enlargement works. Called in Classical times Icosium, legend has it that the town was founded by twenty companions (in Greek *elkosi*) of Hercules. In the 4th century AD it revolted against the Roman occupation and soon disappeared from history. In the 10th century it was refounded by the Sanhadja Berbers, and when the geographer al-Bakri visited it in the 11th century he found it reasonably flourishing and with Classical remains, even mosaics, still in evidence. Such things may well have been sources of motifs for embroidery, pottery, and so on.

During the Middle Ages the history of Algiers was troubled. Eventually, however, the town was taken by the Spaniards and it was to free themselves from these invaders that the people called in Khairaddin, with the resulting Turkish domination already mentioned. At this period, however, as a result of piracy and the trade route up from Africa, Algiers became the biggest slave market in the Mediterranean – even Caribbean pirates such as Bloody Morgan used Algiers and Rabat to dispose of the slaves taken in the sack of Panama. It was also very wealthy from its trade, principally in gold, ivory and sugar.

Museums

Those who wish to visit collections of costumes and embroideries in Algiers have three basic possibilities.

In the old quarter by the fort of the kasba, there is the Museé des Arts et Traditions Populaires, housed in a pretty palace, the Dar Khadoudja El Amia. Begun in the 16th century, on the ruins of an old *zaouia*, "monastery", it was rebuilt last century by the Dey Hassan for his daughter Khadoudja. It has a representative collection of the old crafts of Algeria, including embroideries.

In the southern part of the city, there is the Bardo Museum, housed in one of the 19th-century villas which were built by the wealthy in the more countrified districts. Here, there is a section of "urban ethnography" in which, against the fairly exuberant décor of the Bardo itself, a reconstruction has been made of traditional Algerian interiors. There is also a useful and attractive display of regional costume.

The National Museum of Classical and Muslim Antiquities has displays of the arts and crafts of Tunisia and Morocco as well as those of Algeria, including a number of fine pieces of embroidery and some splendid examples of Berber weaving. Among them, and of particular interest, there are several of the handsome woven and embroidered burnouses, basically black with coloured decoration, from the High Atlas in Morocco.

The embroideries

Algiers was essentially a pirate city and not surprisingly its material culture, including embroideries, originated from a number of different sources. It was towards Istanbul, however, that all eyes were turned and Algiers embroideries – as opposed to Turkish imitations done in Algeria – most resemble those of Turkey, as well as other styles with heavy Ottoman influence, such as Kos and Yannina.

Constantine was particularly well known for its gold work and Bône for its polychrome silk, but Algiers is associated with two main types, commonly known as red and blue, and purple, from their predominant colours.

The Spanish Benedictine, Diego de Haedo, in the late 16th century, speaks of the embroidery of Algiers, adding:

Algiers motif ¹/₃ size.

> "Very few of the women of Algiers know how to work silk, unless they are renegades or Moors from Spain, who learned in their countries of origin, or else their daughters, whom they have taught. Nevertheless, there are some public workshops kept by Moorish women. The work which is learned there, however, is so coarse and the mistress's work so poorly paid that it is held of very little account."

It is clear from this that there were *ma'allemat* – at this date actually of Andalusian origin – as found elsewhere in North Africa and no doubt the organisation of their schools was very much the same as at Fez or Sfax or Tunis.

It is perhaps worth mentioning that Algerian embroidery was done on a Turkish frame – *gourgaf* – not, as in Spain, on a cushion.

Curtains, bniqa and tanchifa

Oddly enough, only three articles seem to be regularly embroidered in the Algiers style. The curtains, which are much the largest pieces, are made of three sections of embroidery, each around 40 cm × 2.5 m, joined together by an odd number of silk ribbons, generally between nine and fifteen, giving a cumulative width of about 1.80-2.00 m. The ribbon in the centre of each group is generally the widest and they are often imported from France, typically Louis XVI, or else of that type. It should be remembered, however, that the original ribbons may have worn out and been replaced, and hence are not a very sure method of dating.

Travellers to Morocco in the 18th century mention these curtains, which, like those of Morocco, are thought to have been used principally on the doors into the courtyard, the fine linen allowing light to enter and the embroidery preventing passers-by from looking in. De Tassy, writing early in the 18th century, says: "At the windows and doors they have curtains of very light cloth, with coloured silk ribbons between the two panels…" and in 1789 Venture de Paradis tells us: "Throughout the kingdom of Algiers large quantities of ribbons are used up in the decoration of furnishings and of women's clothes…For example a curtain made of two panels of material will have in the centre three ribbons of different colours to which these panels will be joined." This sounds like the Moroccan curtains – a pair joined by a central band, but the Algerian curtains which have survived are, I believe invariably, made in three parts.

This bniqa used for wrapping the hair in the bath, and, although the colours are predominantly red and blue, the style is much more that of a purple work. The long strip would originally have been sewn up by folding the central motif (below) in half and sewing it together along its lower edge to make a little cap and tails. Probably Algiers, 18th century

Another of the standard embroidered pieces from Algiers is the *bniqa*, which measures around 15-25 cm by 1.90-2.50 m. It was folded in half and then a small section of one side was sewn up to make a kind of hood with the seam at the back and two long tails. After the bath, it was worn on the head and the tails were wrapped round the hair to dry it. The borders and ends of the *bniqa* are generally richly embroidered – not infrequently with a good deal of gold – and there is also a semi-circular or, sometimes, semi-hexagonal panel in the centre which corresponds to the "cap" when the strip is sewn up. Often this seam has come undone or been unpicked. Sometimes the whole piece is embroidered in very fine gold thread and has flowers in pink, plum, pale blue and other colours to provide relief. Similarly work very occasionally occurs from Tétouan. Analogous caps, intended for everyday and not bath wear, generally gold embroidered and often made of silk or velvet, are found in other cities in Algeria and also in Tunisia, where they are known as *kufiya* – coif.

Haedo mentions these caps, writing in the late 16th century, and calls them *benika*, adding that "they are worked in front in green, yellow or red silk". Clearly, and not surprisingly, in Algiers at least, tastes in colour changed between the 16th and 18th centuries, the most modern preference tends to be for plain gold.

The third piece, called *tanchifa* is, like the *bniqa*, said to have been used in the *hammam* for women to wrap up their heads. As has been explained in the section on Turkish Embroidery, very elegant bathing equipment was normal for well-to-do women in the Muslim world at this time. The *tanchifa* is usually around 30-40 cm × 2.60 m and is generally more heavily embroidered than the *bniqa*, often in horizontal bands or panels along its entire length. Sometimes white or gold and white "ribbons" of open-work alternate with the embroidery on the purple examples, although on the red and blue ones they are limited to the ends, if they occur at all. There may also be silk and gold fringes at the short ends; the same is true of the *bniqa*.

All the main pieces from Algiers, then, are long narrow strips, and it is common to find single curtain panels separated from their fellows. Oddly enough there is very little else in these styles of embroidery and the few anomalous pieces seem as a rule to have been cut down from, presumably damaged, larger ones. It has been suggested that some of the larger strips may have been used for draping over doors, mirrors and so on, as in the case of the Tétouan *tensifas*.

Red and blue

Red and blue are the colours which predominate in a number of pieces, the earliest of which are thought to go back to the 17th century, although of course 18th- and early 19th-century examples are more common. They are worked on a fine, loosely-woven linen and the predominating stitch is brick stitch worked at a slant, known in Arabic as *ma'alka*, with some satin stitch. In the later examples a wider range of stitches is used. The embroidery silk appears to be dyed with natural colours, the blue probably indigo and the red madder or kermes. Although, according to the late 18th-century traveller Venture de Paradis, the people of Algiers were known for their scarlet and purple dyed ribbons, which, he tells us, were considered superior to those of Christendom, they imported their embroidery silks from Marseilles and were sold poor quality stuff. Be that as it may, these red and blue embroideries have kept their colours splendidly, often through a couple of centuries or so.

*   *   *

My daughter is on the swing dressed in her scarlet
caftan.
They have sent for her cousin that he may come
in time.
He will offer a hundred and a hundred pieces of
gold and Aleppo pearls.
He will give a hundred and a hundred pieces of
gold and a black woman to raise the children.

*   *   *

The favourite design on the red and blue embroideries is the artichoke or pomegranate shape so predominant in Turkish art – on Iznik tiles as well as in embroideries within the Ottoman Empire and also in related areas such as Central Asia. It is in fact a pattern which spread all over the Mediterranean in the 15th century and is found on the velvets and brocades from Venice, Genoa and Spain. Indeed, as A.J.B. Wace points out in his survey of Mediterranean embroidery: "Sometimes a real doubt exists as to whether a given textile is of Turkish or Italian origin." In the case of embroideries, this is rarely true – although some of the pieces from Azemmour in Morocco cannot easily be distinguished from their Italian counterparts – but it is hard to tell whether the artichoke motif favoured at Algiers and again at Tétouan is a Spanish or a Turkish contribution – probably the latter.

Detail of Algerian red and blue work from a curtain panel, 18th century

The long strips embroidered with a band of "artichokes" or medallions are generally panels from curtains. In general the earlier pieces have half a dozen or so of these elements enclosed in a border. In the later pieces, the medallions spread into the border, which may even be eliminated, and the bottom medallion tends to become rectangular and fill the entire space.

The more lightly embroidered pieces are generally the *bniqa* and *tanchifa* which have been discussed before.

Purple

Purple — really light or dark violet is the predominant colour in the second type of Algerian embroidery; the source of the dye is not known with any certainty. It has been suggested that the purple pieces are a later development than the red and blue, beginning in the 18th century and continuing until well into the 19th. One reason for this is that although the earliest pieces are on the same loosely woven linen already mentioned, there are also examples on a more closely woven linen, and even on quite ordinary cotton, which are clearly more recent. This progression, or rather degeneration, is not found with the other type. It is commonly believed that the purple work is less fine than the red and blue, although the best pieces are certainly on a similar level of craftsmanship and I personally consider the purple embroidery both more interesting and more elegant.

The purple embroidery is much less solidly worked than the red and blue. Typically there are bands of floreate scrolls outlined in double running stitch and filled in with the very distinctive eyelet holes – called Algerian Eye Stitch, Turkish Star Stitch and in Arabic *zeliledj* – producing a very attractive chequered effect, rather like a fritillary. Some of the scrolls may be worked in solid satin, double darning or brick stitch and scattered through the design are generally very stylized little flowers in delicate colours, which provide a delightful contrast. Touches of gold thread and small gold sequins are sometimes added, especially on the *bniqa*. The purple embroideries in general show a wider range of stitches than the red and blue ones, but those which have a large number of stitches, including, for example, herring bone and laid and couched work, as well as the more traditional ones mentioned above, date from after the coming of the French in 1830.

As with the red and blue pieces, the curtains, which are rare, are generally embroidered in solid strips while the other pieces are principally decorated around the edges and at the ends. A method of dating the purple embroideries by their designs has not yet been established.

Modern embroidery

As in other countries in North Africa, the Service de l'Artisanat has made efforts to preserve the traditional arts and to train new craftsmen. Unfortunately, nothing has been produced on the level of the pieces just described and as far as I have been able to discover, there is no-one in Algiers today capable of doing this kind of embroidery. The small tablecloths and other household items of an eminently saleable nature still made are generally in fairly standard geometric patterns with a considerable admixture of European elements. Gold embroidery has always been a speciality of Algiers and C. Ougouag-Kezzal in his article describes a family of ladies who continue to do this kind of work for their own pleasure. Interestingly enough, they were of Smyrnan origin.

End of a very fine 18th century Algerian piece, showing the 'rivers' of needle wearing. This is probably a bniqa

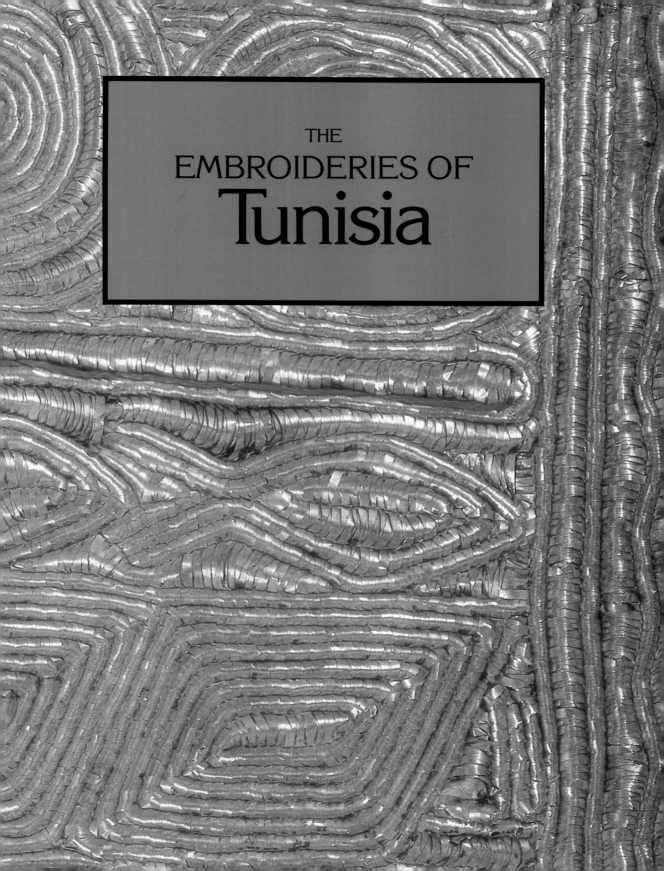

THE
EMBROIDERIES OF
Tunisia

Introduction

The question of Tunisian embroidery is rather different from that of Moroccan, since a great deal of the most interesting work was done on clothes. It is therefore necessary to say a little about costume and because the best pieces are, as is often the case, connected with weddings, a little about the marriage ceremony. Again, since Tunisian symbolism is very homogeneous, not only from town to town, but also from period to period (many of the favourite motifs go back to classical times) and indeed from craft to craft, I have added a short list of the more important ones, while others are discussed in the text as they occur.

Costume

In this book, it is obviously not possible to discuss the very complicated (and fascinating) question of Tunisian costume. Those who would like to know more would be well advised to consult the excellent and admirably illustrated work *Les Costumes Traditionels Feminins de Tunisie*, henceforth cited as *C.T.F.T.*, which has a very complete glossary and a useful bibliography. Interesting articles on many aspects of Tunisian dress, past and present, are to be found in the *Cahiers des Arts et Traditions Populaires* (see bibliography). Those who are interested in the development of costume in North Africa should look at G. Marçais *Le costume Musulman d'Algiers*, which is a most intelligent study, relevant in part also to Tunisia and Morocco.

Draped and sewn

"One protects oneself from the heat and cold by covering one's body with a web of threads forming a cloth. The Bedouin go no further. But the civilized people of the cities cut the material into pieces large enough to cover their bodies and limbs; then sew them together with thread to make a suitable piece of clothing – this is the art of the tailor."

Ibn Khaldun, *Muqqadima.*

Previous page: detail from Moknine wedding tunic.

As we have already discussed in the Introduction, there is a difference between the weaving and the embroidering areas of North Africa, so, at least in Tunisia, there is (or was traditionally – things of course are now changing) a difference between the areas where draped clothes are worn and those where clothes are cut and sewn. There is a further difference between lengths of cloth which are simply folded and sewn up the sides – such as the tunics of Mahdia – and robes which are shaped, such as the Turkish-influenced caftans of Hammamet; a distinction already observed in the 14th century by the great Arab historian born at Tunis, Ibn Khaldun.

The cut and sewn area was, as might be expected, along the coast, roughly from Tunis to Sfax. The rest of the country wore draped clothing and this would once have been essentially true of the men (tunic and *haik*) as well as the women. There is an area running approximately from Sousse to Sfax and inland roughly to El Djem, or a little further, where both types of clothing were habitually used.

There are several ways of wearing the draped dress. The most common in Tunisia is that with a fold at the waist, shin-length, the cloth being held by two large brooches and a belt. Extraordinarily elegant and archaic – the women look like Tanagra figurines – is the manner of certain areas of the far south, where the draperies reach the ankles and one end of the length of cloth is thrown over the head. Odette du Puigaudeau, in her marvellous series of articles (see bibliography) on the people of the Shingit and Walata region of the Sahara, describes the women's dress, which is in the same tradition. There it is known as *chandora* (compare the Iranian *chadur*) from Chandor on the West Coast of India, whence it was originally imported. She adds the curious detail that indigo-dyed cloth was preferred and that the wealthier women would only wear a length for as long as the colour continued to come off slightly on their skins, lending them a bluish lustre, after which the material was considered worn out and would be given away and another piece bought. In the island of Djerba too the long draped dress is worn, but it is held with a single pin.

As might be expected, the makers of the draped dresses are often splendid weavers – but typically not great embroiderers. There are exceptions to this as we shall see. For example, the elaborately patterned woven silk *beskri* of Djerba are also embroidered and there are the strange wool embroidered "veils" of El Djem – a very rare example of an embroidery style apparently coming up from the south out of the Sahara, instead from across the Mediterranean.

Influences

Embroidery, then, is mostly urban and mostly to be found on clothes which are cut and sewn. It is not possible to disentangle the origins of styles as has been done rather successfully for Morocco by Mme Guérard, possibly because in Tunisia the tradition has existed longer and has been more fully absorbed, and also because the Tunisian coast has been much wider open to the culture of the Mediterranean generally. The influences are also rather different, since for geographical reasons contacts have tended to be with Italy and Egypt, rather than Greece. The result of this is that its embroidery has a very mixed origin, although with strong Andalusian and Turkish elements.

One word of caution should perhaps be said: there is a tendency in all North Africa, but especially Tunisia, to attribute anything particularly nice to Andalusia — food, architecture, music, scent, embroidery. Andalusia was, it is true, the cultural heir of Baghdad and so gained a glamour which somehow lasted down through the centuries. This is understandable, but not quite fair. The Turks were already in Tunisia before most of the Andalusians arrived — yet outside Tunis, Istanbul is not much regarded or cited as the *arbiter elegantiae* of the past.

In addition to the Spaniards and Turks, many other nationalities who traded, conquered or came to North Africa as slaves played a part, as the language, rich in loan words, bears witness. If the French gave North Africa the blouse — *bluza*, and shared the chemise — *qamisa*, they perhaps borrowed skirts (*jupes*) — *jebba*, while the Italians, looking at the top rather than the bottom of the same piece of clothing, got jackets (*giubba*), and left behind *malf*, originally from Amalfi, the standard woollen cloth from which most woollen *jebbas* were made.

Marriage

Not surprisingly, the finest clothes were associated with weddings and it is on these rather than on ceremonial robes (as in China) or on children's clothes (as in Italy and Spain) that the best embroidery done this century is to be found. It is also traditional for the bridal (or, especially in Turkey, circumcision) chamber to be hung with embroideries, in other regions with examples of the bride and her family's weaving — indeed kelims and covers and also fine robes and tunics would be used to embellish the entire house. In certain areas — again this tended to be a Turkish custom — special cloths would be embroidered to protect the girl's lap and similarly bags for her to put her hands in while the henna dried. The latter can still be bought at traditional haberdashery or beauty shops in any Tunisian town, or, of course, in the souk. In some areas (see Tétouan, p.79) equivalent "shoulder pieces" were used to protect the bride's robes from oily scents and pomades when her hair was ritually dressed before the marriage ceremony. At Sfax, the hennaing — which is lengthy — took place to the accompaniment of three women singing and playing tambourines, or other instruments.

The third day — Jelwa

The third day was the marriage proper, with the exchange of contracts and registry of the dowry at the house of the bride's family.

In the afternoon came the *jelwa*, or the ceremony of the presentation of the bride. The rite is said to go back to Abbasid times and even to have had a counterpart in Classical Greece. Essentially it involves the girl showing herself veiled then unveiled first to her own relatives, then to the connections of the groom. She usually has to walk and move, and at some stage stand with her hands uplifted in the very ancient position of the orante, or supplicant, which, it should not be forgotten, is also one of the gestures of Muslim prayer. It is maintained that the bride shows herself off in this way so that it can be seen by many witnesses that she has no outward imperfections. There is also, of course, the idea of showing off her beauty, all the more so since for many weeks or months before she will have dressed with great plainness, so that on the day of *jelwa* "she may appear like the full moon emerging from behind the clouds."

Bride in the position of jelwa, *stylized in a way very similar to Tanit on the Carthaginian steles. Tanit has the crescent moon above her head and holds ears of corn; the bride has the full moon and seems to scatter grain — Gabès.*

At Sfax the *jelwa* takes a very particular form. The bride, dressed in seven tunics worn one on top of the other, goes up on to a dais. She is ritually unveiled and displayed to the guests. Then, with her hands raised, she gyrates so that those present can see her from all sides. Afterwards, she retires to a room set apart for the purpose, removes her outer tunic and returns. This is repeated seven times until at last she appears in her most splendid tunic, and sits on a kind of throne, her face again veiled and her hands on her breasts.

Possibly this rite, or some ancient version of it, was the origin of the Dance of the Seven Veils, which the Western imagination interpreted for some reason as strip-tease. I also do not know why it is associated with Salome: "But when Herod's birthday was kept, the daughter of Herodias danced before them, and pleased Herod." *Matthew:* 14 v. 6.

In other towns, the gestures of the *jelwa* are somewhat different. At Djerba, for example, the bride alternately places her hands

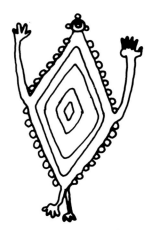

Bride in the jelwa *position embroidered in concentric rows of fine silk thread on a headdress from Bekalta. One of three such figures standing among fish, flowers, suns and stars. These extraordinary stylizations of the human figure are reminiscent of those at Tassili in the Sahara.*

on her eyes and extends them palms out and fingers extended towards the on-lookers to avert the evil eye.

* * *

"In the long echoing street the laughing dancers throng
The bride is carried to the bridegroom's chamber through torchlight and tumultuous song..."

from *Oedipus at Colonus* translated by W.B. Yeats

* * *

The next ritual is no longer practised in urban Sfax as a matter of course, nor generally in the Sahel, but is still important in the south. The bride, laden with jewels, is set in a beautifully decorated *jehfa* or camel-litter and carried through the streets to the bridegroom's house, accompanied by singers beating tambourines and the ululations of the women. Her dowry, consisting largely of clothes and linen, is loaded on a mule to form part of the procession. In Sfax, however, a car with white ribbons is generally substituted for the camel and the honking of car horns for the tambourines.

The *jelwa* is then repeated at the house of the bridegroom before selected relatives and guests. After this, and further ceremonies, including prayer, the marriage is consummated.

The sixth day

This is marked in Sfax by the ceremony called Jumping over the Fish – *nhar tangiz ala el-hut.* The bride, dressed in a purple caftan (of the kind described for Hammamet, but without a belt) and a red jacket, covered with jewels and wearing embroidered high-heeled slippers, jumps seven times over a tray of large fish decked with flowers – a rite intended to ensure good luck and fertility. In Europe, the throwing of rice or confetti (the latter presumably borrowed from Italy and apparently misunderstood – flower petals should be thrown and *confetti*, sugared almonds or other sweetmeats, distributed to the by-standers for luck) or the bride tossing her bouquet or her garter is perhaps comparable.

The seventh day

Slipping from her waist, half untied,
Her sixty-fold belt
Not of wool, but all embroidered with silver,
A he-camel and a she-camel I paid for it.

*   *   *

In Sfax this is not, apparently, much celebrated, but in many other towns the ceremony of *tahzim* – Putting on the Belt – is an essential ritual. All over North Africa, as in the Classical World and indeed in Mediaeval Europe, belts had immense symbolic importance. In North Africa it was (and is) generally felt that the bride should not wear a belt, which is essential for holding together the draped dress, and the custom necessitating, therefore, the marriage tunic – from the Night of Henna until well after the consummation of the marriage, and the most commonly given explanation is that it would "bind" her and impede conception.

On the seventh day (although it may be the third or the fifth) she resumes the belt and the rite also indicates her returning to normal or "real" life. It is put on her sometimes by her mother-in-law, sometimes by a relative who has male children, in the presence of at least one and sometimes many little boys, to ensure that she will have sons. This belt is carefully kept throughout her life and during childbirth it is fixed to the wall for her to pull on – popular belief maintaining that it links her symbolically to Fatima, the daughter of Muhammad and the mother of Hassan and Hussein.

It is also said, at other places besides Sfax, that a girl who ties her belt before the seventh day will dominate her husband.

As might be expected, these belts throughout North Africa are often very sumptuous and precious. They are, however, usually woven (although the Bedouin and the Berbers in particular have all kinds of plaited and macramé versions) and, except for the gold embroidered belts of the type used Hammamet and discussed in the section on Fez, embroidery is only used as a subsidiary form of decoration. Indeed, it should be remembered that fine weaving requires the most time and skill and therefore is the most prized textile technique, with embroidery as a relatively cheap substitute. Printing or painting on cloth, of course, stand lowest of all.

Lending and renting

It might be thought, in view of the immense value of the wedding clothes, that only the very rich could afford to get married in style. This is of course partly true – a poor family obviously cannot manage the celebrations that a rich one can – but not entirely.

Firstly, families are prepared to spend a much higher proportion of their incomes than might be expected on celebrating the major events of life and even go into debt in order to do so. Also, in the past, when the clothes were made at home, they would be worked on and accumulated gradually over many years.

Secondly, there is the possibility of renting. This is, in fact, becoming increasingly the norm as fewer and fewer women actually make their own wedding clothes and as the prices of the raw materials soar. Thus, families which possess fine sets of robes or hangings can do quite well out of renting them. This practice is further discussed in the section on Tunis.

Thirdly, there is the possibility of borrowing. Of course, this was always common within a family, but it was also considered an act of charity to lend precious robes and jewels for such an occasion and one which brought divine reward. To refuse if asked would be thought to run counter to the Koran: "Misfortune... on those who refuse help, succour." S.107/v. 4-7, but to offer, especially to a poor girl or to an orphan, is held yet more auspicious – and this is surely very ancient.

In some cities, for example Bizerte, it was the custom for the bride to borrow the chemise she would wear on her wedding night from an older woman – and the case of one particularly lucky one which had served seven brides is cited. It is said that elsewhere, a well-to-do woman without children would lend her robes and jewels to orphan girls in the hopes that they would come back to her impregnated with *baraka* – blessing, so that she would conceive. In this case, one wonders whether there was not an element of trying to transfer her ill-luck – and whether the poorer girl was simply grateful for the generous offer, or whether she feared the "eye".

Symbols

In Tunisia, very much the same range of symbols is found across all the arts – embroidered, carved on stone door frames, painted on dower chests and wall-brackets, or on the paintings on glass which are a local speciality, glazed on plates and bowls, and so on.

Many of the symbols are very old – the crescent and the star, as we have already said, are not only the emblem of Islam, but also appear on Punic grave stele, while the hand, and the Tree of Life are among the oldest symbols there are. Other motifs are clearly classical—or at least their modern stylizations can be paralleled with examples from the classical period; the motifs themselves may be earlier still.

Some of them are curious to our eyes. The scissors, for example, embroidered at the neck of a marriage tunic or appearing as a graffito on the amphitheatre of El Djem, might to us suggest the shears of Atropos and hence, at least for a wedding, be most unsuitable. In fact, the scissors, which are probably pruning shears, but also suggest those used for circumcision and are hence a fertility symbol, since it is widely believed that just as a vine will not fruit well unless pruned, so…I have had this offered to me as the explanation for the small size of "Christian" families! The stylisation of the scissors, by the way, is definitely phallic.

There are also some surprising omissions. The horse, for example is very rare, although the horses of the Barbary Coast — "barbs" — were famous, while the camel is found everywhere, even outside the areas where they are especially common. It must be assumed that the horse was never of much importance to ordinary people — their luxury beast being the camel for literary and historic as much as for practical reasons. Another example: the peacock—a very powerful symbol all round the Mediterranean is, of course, not indigenous, yet extremely common, while the cock, usually a favourite folk motif, and one with special associations in Islam, is very rare except on some of the wool embroideries from El Djem and the South.

One more creature, which I have never seen embroidered, although it is a favourite subject of glass-painting, is Buraq, the mule with the face of a woman and tail of a lion, on which Muhammad made the "Night Journey" to Jerusalem, according to tradition. This is perhaps less surprising, since Buraq is a literary and therefore slightly "academic" creature and so more likely as a subject to appeal to men rather than women.

Tunisian embroidery is rather more naturalistic than Moroccan, but nevertheless, apart from certain wool embroideries, such as those of El Djem, the stylizations are very predictable and urban, in the sense that they were evolved in the cities (at least in this Islamic cycle of their existence) and copied by the villagers, rather than being observed direct from nature. There are rare exceptions, but this is the rule.

Generally speaking, however, Tunisian symbols are remarkably consistent throughout the country and throughout the centuries; here are some of the more important ones, which may be studied in greater breadth and depth in *Signes et Symboles dans l'Art Populaire Tunisien* (see bibliography).

Birds

These are among the most popular subjects, particularly in embroidery, glass painting and on dower chests, and, usually in pairs, they are very naturally connected with marriage. The favourites are doves – associated in antiquity with the cults of Tanit and Aphrodite, and often curiously similar to their Carthaginian counterparts – and peacocks, which are discussed in the section on Azemmour in Morocco. Either species may be shown flanking a bowl or vase, perhaps suggesting the Water of Life, or else a basket of fruit and flowers – the Tree of Life, conceivably? It should be stressed that the embroideresses themselves certainly do not give these rather sophisticated meanings to their work.

Birds at a flower vase originally representing the tree of life – couched gilt silver thread outlines with sequin infill. Often this motif is shown with peacocks or doves drinking at a bowl and the first reference to it is a description by Pliny of a famous mosaic at Pergamon in Asia Minor. It became one of the most popular subjects throughout the classical and on into the Christian world. There is also a version with swimming fishes – Tunis.

On a bridal dress in the Musée de Moknine, there is a very charming couched gold embroidery of a dove sitting on her nest, but this is a less common theme than one might expect. Rare, too, as has been said, is the cock, and I have seen just one piece from the south with what might have been an ostrich – although they have been extinct in Tunisia for some time. Once it must have been a common motif as it was a common image, and not only to the nomads:

> "We passed Tripoli, the scented, city of merchants,
> She is, I swear it, like a she-ostrich guarding her
> eggs."

sang a reciter of the Romance of the Beni Hilal at Takrouna as late as the 1920s.

The camel

The camel, like the palm, is an image deeply rooted in Islamic symbolism. Unlike the birds, this is not an urban image, but a rural one, and mostly found in the south. The covers and kelims of Gafsa have the camel as a favourite motif — after all it is one of the commonest animals there and indicative of wealth and abundance, besides having specific associations with the marriage — it is often represented carrying the bride in a decorated litter. The camel again appears on the "veils" of El Djem, which are somewhat aberrant in the context of Tunisian embroideries; and of course on the pottery of the South as well as, now, on all sorts of objects intended for the tourist market.

The eye

The eye is not at all a common symbol in embroidery, although the fish is sometimes stylized in such a way to suggest it, but it is a very important concept in North African folk art. As in Italy and elsewhere, the eye, the 'ain, usually the product of envy, is much feared and efforts of all kinds are made to counteract it. These range from prayers and the frequent calling on the name of God, to careful forms of courtesy and charms and spells. Many of the embroideries on marriage robes, especially the fish and the hand, are not only good-luck symbols, but are also intended to protect the girl from envy and malice on her "day of days". The golden robe of "the eye against the eye" is mentioned in the section on Nabeul, and amulets in the form of an eye are found everywhere throughout the Middle East, particularly pinned on babies' clothes.

One prophylactic symbol is the horn, which puts out the "evil eye" and is sometimes found in both embroidery and weaving; a pair of horns may also be set on the roof of the house for the same reason in certain areas, for example at La Marsa.

Two horns also, of course, suggest the crescent moon and furthermore Alexander the Great, an important figure in Islamic mythology, who is always known as Dhu'l Karnein – Possessor of the Two Horns. The beautiful hill to the right looking out across the bay of Tunis is Bou Kornein – the Father of the Two Horns. These things have no doubt worked together to make the horns a particularly important local symbol, although they figure commonly in all Mediterranean superstition. In Italy, the phrase and gesture to avert misfortune – *facciamo i corni*, or let us make horns accompanied by the extending of little and first finger, serves the same purpose and is in effect the negative version of the English – let us keep our fingers crossed.

The fish

Me and my wool – a fish on us!
Ben Salah awaits.
Oh spindle unequalled!
I shall earn with you 1000 riyals.

*   *   *

Fish in gilt silver thread with sequin scales – urban Tunisia.

No symbol is so strikingly Tunisian as the fish. It is literally everywhere – from the dried fish tail hung from the driving mirror and the little paper fish stuck to the portable radio (to prevent the batteries running down? to protect it from being stolen?) to the beautifully painted dower chests of last century, where three fish tails often share one head, making a triangle with a single eye, or the rows of fish swimming along a cover or a kelim in the south. Everywhere in the souk strings of velvet fish decorated with flowers, hands and perhaps the name of God in gold paper or embroidery are offered for sale, and if you stop at an ordinary stall or restaurant for some couscous or soup, there will probably be a fish painted on the bottom of the bowl. The women of Cap Bon pin five fish eyes to their children's clothes (an interesting combination of the fish and hand motifs, which are indeed very often associated) and it is still customary to bury a fish by the door for good luck – a dim echo of the threshold fish mosaics of the past, or, more probably both reflect the same very persistent belief. At a more modern sophisticated level, the advertisements put out by a Tunisian bank to encourage the opening of savings accounts were at one time fish-shaped and the accounts themselves were called *El Khadra* – green, a colour considered to be of great auspiciousness.

It is hardly surprising that the teeming seas off the Tunisian coast, portrayed in numerous Roman mosaics, should have suggested the idea of fertility, certainly from Carthaginian times and doubtless earlier; and the fish sometimes becomes a phallic symbol, particularly when it swims downwards, holding a string of smaller fish in its mouth. This ancient liking for the fish was no doubt reinforced during Tunisia's Christian period (Christianity survived in places until the 10th century), for the fish was associated with Christ the Saviour. Interestingly, there are Coptic ceramics, for example a 7th-century plate from Sakkarah, now in the Louvre, which has fish and birds portrayed almost exactly as they appear on ordinary Tunisian earthenware today, and even the shape with its pie-crust edge is similar. Again, fish are a favourite Coptic textile motif, for example on the well-known Tapestry of the Fish, of 2nd-3rd century from Antinoe.

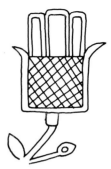

All in all, it is hardly surprising that scarcely a marriage costume should have been made without a fish embroidered somewhere, although they are often very stylized and have to be disentangled from leaves and curlicues, especially in cities such as Tunis and Bizerte, where the Muslim prohibition on portraying living things was taken to heart more than in countryside.

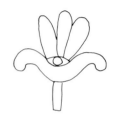

A last point: fish appear in all kinds of auspicious phrases, the most common being *hut ala al-rasak* — a fish on your head — indicating may you have good luck, may all go well with you.

The hand

The hand, as has already been noted, is one of the oldest prophylactic symbols in the world, probably going back to the palaeolithic age, and is found all round the Mediterranean and throughout the Islamic world. Known to Westerners as the Hand of Fatima, it is called in Arabic *khomsa* — having five — and appears literally everywhere. It carries suggestions of prayer and protection — a barrier against the evil eye and also of being in the hand of God; besides which, five is held to be a lucky number. This superstition has been rationalized in various ways — there are five pillars of Islam, five daily prayers and so on. It also said that the predilection derives from the Roman five — V — which suggests the horn which pierces the "eye".

Three stylizations of the hand-khomsa. From Tunis in metal thread, disguised as a flower to avoid charges of superstition; in heavy flat metal thread, tal, with the "eye against the eye" in the palm and shaped like a lily flower, filled in with lines of silk embroidery and accompanied by the fish, symbol of fertility.

Sometimes the stylization of the hand is phallic, with the index alone extended, but much more often it becomes a kind of flower, a lily, as was already the case on certain Phoenician stele. It may also be so formal as to be almost unrecognizable, for example in certain pieces of weaving, showing the very old garden pattern, where the ends of the crosses are hands, a single flower appears in each quarter and the fish have become diamonds. The hand and the fish very frequently appear in association and sometimes an eye on the palm is added.

The tree

Palm tree embroidered in green and yellow silk; the circles represent gilt silver sequins. It is flanked by figures and stands in a field of brightly coloured flowers – Sfax.

Floral and plant motifs are among the most common in Tunisian art, urban and rural, partly because they are exempt from the ban on portraying living things, and partly because they are the obvious form of decoration for people whose livelihood depends on the fertility of the soil. Curiously, although like everyone else, the Tunisians obviously think flowers are pretty, there is no great interest in them, in the sense that the Turks were interested in various aspects of horticulture and even flower arranging. As in Morocco, the flowers are extremely stylized and by-and-large unrecognisable except, again, where there has been Turkish influence, or rather, where the pieces actually *are* Turkish or direct copies. Clearly what was important was the idea of flowering and a pleasing effect, rather than representation of an actual plant which the embroideress had before her eyes. Given the splendour of the spring flowers over much of North Africa, especially in the hills and along such fertile areas as the coast of Cap Bon, this would seem to show an extraordinary lack of imagination, but this is the norm for peasant embroideries and is the general rule all round the Mediterranean.

As regards trees, too, the situation is odd. The olive, which has always had a very important place in Tunisia's economy, never appears in the art of the Muslim period, although it was common in Classical times. The trees depicted are the palm – a powerful symbol throughout Islam – so characteristic of the south, and the cypress, rare in Tunisia, although beloved of Italy and Turkey; from the latter it was no doubt copied.

The trees and, by extension, the vases and compositions of flowers, undoubtedly trace their ancestry back to the Tree of Life, another very old motif, omnipresent in the Mediterranean – and beyond. The embroideresses of the Sahel or of Raf-Raf were almost certainly never aware of its significance – unlike the hand or the fish, it was simply a pleasant, auspicious, time-honoured subject.

Cypress tree couched in thick natural silk thread from the breast of a man's robe – Tunis.

The woman

Naceur Baklouti, writing the section on anthropomorphic motifs in *Signes et Symboles dans l'Art Populaire Tunisien*, observes very perceptively that the human figure, which is rare in Tunisian art, appears almost exclusively in those crafts which are practised by women: embroidery, weaving and pottery (as opposed to wood, stone and metal work, which are the province of men) in the country rather than the towns, and in the hinterland rather than along the coast. This, of course, corresponds to the section of the population least affected by the prohibition on representing the human figure, which has been mentioned before.

The figures on kelims and pottery may be male or female, while those in embroidery are almost invariably women, probably because of their close connection with marriage and the bride. Generally very schematic, the figures tend to be geometric rather than curvilinear – this is perhaps connected to the strength of the weaving which normally, at least in thickish wools, produces straight rather than curved lines. A good example is the completely geometric figure known in the Matmata as Djazia, after the beautiful and warlike heroine of the Romance of the Beni Hilal.

Commonly the little figure has her hands raised in the classic position of *jelwa* – which is, however, also reminiscent of Tanit, the fertility goddess of ancient North Africa, who appears in this position (also, stylized as a triangle with a round head as in a child's drawing) on steles from Carthage, sometimes with horns or the crescent moon above her head and with palm branches in her hands.

On the "veils" from El Djem, there are sometimes figures from the marriage procession, including the bride in her camel litter and the *jelwa*, but there are also strange creatures looking as if they come from outer space, which may again be anthropomorphic; it is hard to tell. Similar beings appear on the embroideries from Gabès.

Other types of embroidery

The kind of embroidery dealt with in the following sections is largely the silk, cotton and wool needlework done by women, and to a lesser extent the local styles of gold embroidery. The urban silver and gold thread and sequin embroidery, which is in fact made in many of the larger towns, is described in the section on Tunis and is fairly standard. The heavier gold embroidery and embroidery on leather used for saddles and saddlery is mostly done by men and is not covered in detail in this book, although there is some information on them under Gold Embroideries of Fez and there are several suggestions for further reading in the bibliography. Again, this kind of embroidery, heavily influenced by Turkey, is comparatively uniform all along the North African coast in the main centres, such as Rabat, Algiers, Tunis, and Tripoli, and indeed in Cairo and round the Eastern Mediterranean as well.

Even the descriptions given here of the silk, cotton and wool embroidery are very far from comprehensive. Tunisia is a country where each village easily evolves an individual style and unfortunately I have not been able to spend long enough there to disentangle all the different traditions (the fact that many of them now belong to the past does not make it easier) or even the work done on all the different pieces of clothing. Among headdresses, for example, the *qufiya* (coif) of Korba is quite different from that of Bekalta or from the *duka* of Sousse, or the *bint duka* (daughter of the *duka,* which looks very like the Venetian doge's cap) and all carry quite distinctive embroideries; but, once more, this is not really the place to go into them in any detail – there is an excellent article by Clémence Sugier (see bibliography). What I have tried to do is to provide some guide to the main types and, I hope, some more serious scholar, perhaps working on the very nice collection at the Centre des Arts et Traditions Populaires at Carthage will produce a more exhaustive work before it is too late and before too many of the pieces have vanished entirely.

One peculiarity of Tunisia is that while small places such as Moknine or Raf-Raf produce very recognisable embroidery, large urban centres, for example Bizerte and Sousse, do not. This is for the simple reason that their styles, insofar as they ever had any, became absorbed by the capital which they imitated, while in the poorer, more isolated place this did not occur. A few words should, however, be said about the embroidery of these major towns:

Bizerte

There has been a city on the site of Bizerte since the 4th century BC, when it was known as Hippo Acra. Generally it has been walled – Agathocles, Belisarius and Charles V being among those who rebuilt the fortifications. As a result of this, the city has always stood apart from the Bedouin and Berbers of the surrounding countryside, linked culturally to the other urban centres of North Africa rather than to its own hinterland. It is perhaps for this reason that Bizerte, although large and important, has no real style of its own, but has traditionally borrowed that of Tunis, which is very easily reached. Certainly, in embroidery there is no specifically Bizerte work. The town did, of course, have its own costumes, particularly embroidered leggings, *swiqat*, which were a common feature of North African urban dress (see Fez) and were said to originate in Andalusia – although 18th-century travellers in the Greek Islands comment on the ugliness of the women's embroidered "leg warmers" which made their calves and ankles look very thick, so the fashion may have come from there.

Kairouan

Since it is the most important religious centre in North Africa and often counted after Mecca, Medina and Jerusalem as the fourth Holy City of Islam, it is surprising that Kairouan should have no very distinctive dress. It is firmly within the draped dress/weaving area, which perhaps explains the lack of embroidery, but this was not always the case, for very early Maghribi gold-embroidered carpets are mentioned as luxury objects at Baghdad. The term Maghrib (Occident) was then applied to Spain as well as North Africa, but gold Kairouani carpets are mentioned in other contexts. Certainly, Kairouan is a major producer of rugs and kelims today, but, as far as I know, no special gold embroidery is now done there and certainly not on carpets.

There is a fascinating 11th-century letter from Cairo to Kairouan, found in the Cairo *Geniza* (and quoted by S. Goitein, *Letters* pp. 76-77) in which the writer describes *exactly* the clothes he wants to order, and already at that date he specifies "the best robes manufactured are the old ones" – there are other references from this period to "old-style" or antique objects being preferred. The writer goes on to say that he would like a particular type of festival costume (described) and adds very humanly:

> "If you cannot obtain one like that, then it should be red, striped with curved lines, like the robe which Abi Ibrahim Ayyash had made for himself – and I do not care if it costs 1 or 2 dinars more."

Monastir

One of the most important towns of the Sahel, Monastir – as its name suggests – has a long and complex religious history. It is said that the *ribat* (compare, *Rabat*) was built by Harun al-Rashid's most competent captain, Harthema Ibn Ayan. According to the historian al-Idrisi, when the Beni Hilal invaded, devastating the rest of the country, "the Arabs did no harm to the fields and orchards of

Monastir, a sacred place where all antagonisms are neutralized." The result has been that Monastir, rather surprisingly, again belongs to the urban network and its costume and embroidery are not particularly distinctive. It is perhaps worth mentioning the traditional *jelwa* costume is one of the heaviest and most golden of the coast, with very wide shoulders, and broad trousers and sleeves — very concealing, in keeping with the religious tradition of the city, but also to protect the girl at this important moment against the evil eye. The impression of armour which these tunics give may not be entirely coincidental. Together with the make-up and headdress, this Monastir costume has almost the stiff hieratic effect of Japanese Noh robes.

Another town which similarly has a remarkable golden costume is the nearby Ourdanine, where the sleeveless jacket has enormous stiffened epaulettes and hence is called *farmla bej jawanah* — jacket with wings. This is of course, the *jelwa* costume and here the gesture differs from that of Sfax or Djerba — the bride keeps her hands on her breasts.

Sfax

Sfax, again very pleasantly sited on the sea, is the second most important town in Tunisia and has a very long tradition as a merchant city, with particular connections with Egypt and Tripolitania, whence the corsaire Dragut brought forty families who settled in Sfax in the 16th century and influenced its customs.

Sfax is also an important town for crafts, and although its embroidery (largely gold-work) is not distinctive it is fine. The costume, until it was supplanted by the Tunis fashions, consisted of a caftan which reached below the knee leaving the lower part of the leg bare. The neck-line and the bolero jacket were as usual richly decorated with gold. The women of Sfax, as in most towns, although this has barely been mentioned, covered their heads with a mass of embroidered scarves, ribbons and jewels.

Sousse

Sousse has a charming old town and kasba standing by the sea and one of the oldest mosques in Tunisia, now restored. It is a considerable tourist centre. It was particularly prosperous about 100 years ago and presumably at that time lost its own traditions of embroidery in favour of those of Tunis. Like other towns in the area it had a golden *jelwa* costume, in fact two. For the first *jelwa* at her own house, the bride wore a knee-length tunic made of vertical ribbons of gold embroidery alternating with gold brocade and relatively tight trousers, usually gold embroidery on dark green. The bottom part of the trousers was worked in horizontal bands to suggest the embroidered leggings – *swiqat* – (see Bizerte) which had already gone out of use earlier this century. For the second *jelwa* at the groom's house, she wore a wide knee-length caftan again over tightish trousers. In Sousse the prophylactic gesture made by the bride is that of holding the hands horizontal across the breast. It will be noticed that Sousse, a relatively open town, has a rather more revealing costume than that of Monastir.

Learning to embroider

Mistress, teach her a skill, set her to work and
direct her;
The gold ring is on her finger, the silk in her
hands.
Mistress, teach her a skill, set her working for the
Sultan's daughter
You will receive a fattened lamb and a basket
with quintals of dates.
Mistress teach her a skill and set her to work for
the Caïd's daughter
You will receive a fattened lamb and a basket
well-filled with dates.
The mistress spoke two words to me which went
straight to my heart:
Your daughter is careful, her words please me
well.
The mistress spoke two words to me on the
threshold of the house:
Your daughter is careful, her words are worth
gold.
The mistress spoke two words standing under
the eaves:
Your daughter should be veiled, the young men
will come after her.

*   *   *

Rough sketch of a gourgaf

Some details of how embroideresses are trained are given in the sections on Morocco and Tunis – the system is, or was, roughly the same throughout urban North Africa. Sfax had a rather sophisticated version of it, in that the *ma'allema*, or teacher, had a particularly high reputation and might well be of good family, directing work-women and creating fashions. There was even one particularly famous teacher, Zin Masmoudia, who taught her pupils the Koran, besides embroidery. Certain families produced long lines of *ma'allema* who were especially well-regarded.

Traditionally the girls studied with the *ma'allema* between the ages of seven and fifteen, but only during the winter, since in the summer everyone tended to go out into the country. A *ma'allema* might have as many as forty pupils and she would sit among them, with the most competent nearest her, calling them to her to oversee their work. A *ma'allema* was always anxious to get rid of incompetent pupils, since it was by the work of her trained students that she was judged. Conversely, parents especially middle-class ones, would try to move their daughters to more prestigious *ma'allema*. A good deal of competition resulted. The *ma'allema* would be paid a fixed sum each month and in addition would be given presents, often food or cakes, on feast days, marriages in the families of her pupils and similar occasions. There would also be gifts of *halwa* – sweets – and perhaps money on the day the girl completed her first piece of work successfully.

Once trained, the *sanaa*, as the girls were called, would begin to sew for themselves, their families and gradually acquire a clientele. If their work was of high enough quality and their moral standing irreproachable; they would become *ma'allema* in their turn. This was considered very desirable as they would be in a position to help their fathers, and later their husbands, contribute to their trousseaux and, if widowed, support themselves and their children. A *sanaa* had a very definite advantage when it came to marriage. In fact, although the sums paid for each piece of work were, in the past, not great, it was possible for the *ma'allema* to gather an appreciable nest-egg. Goitein in vol. I, p. 128 (see bibliography) tells us that in mediaeval Cairo: "One embroiderer [f.] was rich enough to donate a Torah scroll to a synagogue, another, a Muslim, for buying a house worth 400 dinars." Her counterpart in Sfax would likewise have bought property for preference, or an olive grove, or else jewellery. Again, a recent study showed that the earnings of women working at embroidery, lace, and so on (often for the Artisanat) in the southern areas might constitute as much as a third of the family income. It is hardly surprising that it was – and to some extent still is – so popular an activity.

DJERBA AND KERKENNA

In the name of God, I begin to work you
By the aid of God, I shall complete you.

*   *   *

Djerba

Djerba is said to be the Island of the Lotus Eaters of the Odyssey; it has both Phoenician and Roman remains. According to local tradition, the Jewish population goes back to the destruction of Jerusalem by Nebuchadnezzar in 587 BC, but a more probable date is the lst century AD diaspora of Titus. Over the millennia, it has passed from hand to hand. Its first bishop was appointed in AD 256. Vandals, Byzantines and Arabs succeeded each other. It was devastated by the Beni Hilal; Normans and Aragonese fought over it; Turks took it, building a tower of skulls out of the Spanish garrison, which stood until the 19th century and the coming of the French.

Still as charming as its reputation, Djerba, like all the south, is much better known for its weaving than its embroidery. The best place to get an idea of such needlework as does exist is the Musée des Arts et Traditions Populaires de l'Ile de Djerba, which is housed in the very attractive *zaouia* of Sidi Zitouni. It has, among all sorts of other things, a good collection of costume, very nicely displayed and labelled.

The most striking points about the various costumes of Djerba are firstly the extraordinary elegance with which the long draperies are held by a single brooch, often without a belt, and secondly the beautiful plays of stripes, which are characteristic of the island.

In the name of God! He alone is God!
Oh God, help us and lend us the aid You once
                              gave to Lady Fatima,
Who began a burnous for her father in the
                              morning
And finished it at eventide.

The most splendid lengths of weaving and embroidery were the lengths of silk known as *biskri*, generally made by the Jewish community, used for the draped dress. Typically striped and checked in deep subtle colours with touches of fine gold thread, they were then embroidered over the woven pattern with geometric designs in silk. Favourite motifs, not surprisingly, are the seven-branched candlestick and the seal of Solomon. The men wove and the women embroidered. These were – and are (they are still made to a very limited extent on commission) – luxury objects involving several months' work and hundreds of dinars. (1 Tunisian dinar = approximately £1 in 1983).

A type of embroidery much more similar to that of Gabès is that used to join the two halves of the veil or head-covering – *futa* – which is made of white cotton, sometimes woven with red bands and checks, in summer, and black in winter. Red, yellow and green silk is used to make an embroidered chequerboard along the join and for a narrow border and fringes. It was usual for women to embroider them themselves.

The common type of gold embroidery is also done in Djerba, especially on the bolero jackets, which exist in two styles: Tripolitanian – there is much influence from there – and Tunis, that is with small winged sleeves. The Jewish women also made embroidered head-coverings; as elsewhere in North Africa they were traditionally very strict in observing the Talmudic prohibition on showing their hair (compare the wigs and elaborate headdresses of southern Morocco) using metal thread, which was, however, passed through the cloth itself instead of being couched as in other areas.

The draped dress of Djerba went over a straight tunic, rather in the Roman manner, and this was decorated, much as we have seen elsewhere, with a very pretty plastron of coloured embroidery, vaguely comparable, although without the black work, to those of Nabeul. This was again a speciality of the Jewish women – the Jewish community being intimately connected with the very considerable textile trade and industry of the island.

The original Berber inhabitants of Djerba clung strongly to their language and traditions, but various sects took up their residence there. The results, naturally, was a large number of purely local customs – for example that of not working for fifteen days at Ashura (the commemoration of the death of Muhammad's grandsons) on penalty of getting "the shakes", disastrous, obviously, for an embroiderer or weaver, or during the "blessed days", the seven days between 25th February and 4th March, or on Fridays.

J. and S. Combès, in their article on wool-working in Djerba in 1946, tell the following anecdote:

"An old black woman of the island told us, à propos of this, of a very unpleasant meeting she had had with 'the man with the big turban'.

From childhood she had been a slave at Constantinople and on arriving at Djerba knew nothing of the customs of the island. She therefore set about working wool one Friday morning... Sitting alone in the room, she was absorbed in her work, when suddenly she could no longer see anything – a very old man wearing a large, an enormous turban was standing on the threshold blocking out the daylight. He looked at the black woman for a long moment and then said in a reproachful voice:

> 'Swear it on the head of your grand-father.'
> Three times she was exhorted to give up her
> work. Three times she proffered obedience,
> trembling. At once the old man vanished,
> leaving her much troubled. 'The man with the
> big turban was well aware that I was acting
> out of ignorance, otherwise...!'

And the old woman congratulated herself on having escaped his punishments."

Kerkenna

Kerkenna is, of course, quite different from Djerba, being culturally linked with Sfax rather than Gabès. Unlike Djerba, there is a good deal of embroidery, but unfortunately I have not had the opportunity to go there and consequently know very little about it.

The most important pieces are the two red woollen shawls – *tarf er-ras* (head shawl) and *tarf el-ktef* (shoulder shawl) worn, one over the head and one draped round the body over a tunic – *jebba* – also of red wool. The head-shawl is decorated along its length with geometric motifs in green, orange-red and black wool, and white cotton, and along its short ends with pompoms in the same colours. The patterns are given all sorts of charming names; wedding candles, palanquin of the bride, presentation of the bride, and so on. These motifs, inspired in all likelihood by weaving, are rectilinear, as are the local renderings of the auspicious symbols: birds, fish, palms, jewels. Unusually, the principal stitch tends to be cross-stitch. Traditionally, the best embroideresses were from the Ouled Kasim, but now that the Artisanat has begun to encourage the craft, it has spread to other villages, especially Remla.

The shoulder shawl is very similar, except that the right sides of the two bands are on opposite sides of the material, so that when the upper band is folded over the belt it is right side out not wrong. This is a common arrangement in the Sahel, found in the costume of Ksar Hellal, Moknine and elsewhere.

At some point, Kerkenna borrowed the *sirwal*, or trousers, from Sfax, and in the old days the bottoms were embroidered with the kind of black work found at Mahdia.

EL DJEM

domi mansit, lanam fecit
She stayed home and worked wool

– epitaph of a woman of the Roman republic from
Mezdour (15 km from Monastir)

The great amphitheatre of El Djem, the largest surviving monument in Roman Africa, seems so improbable as it looms up out of the surrounding plain that it suggests a mirage. Probably built under Gordian in AD 238, it is the place where, according to folk tradition, the Berber leader, the Kahina – or Prophetess, she was a kind of North African Boadicea – made her last stand against the Arab invaders. Clustered about the amphitheatre is a small town of some 12,000 inhabitants which has taken the place of the large and wealthy Roman Thysdrus.

The embroidery

Surprisingly – but we have seen this several times – El Djem has an extremely distinctive local embroidery style, one which has little in common with the pretty and formal needlework of the towns, but which suggests a completely different current coming up out of sub-Saharan Africa.

El Djem is an important centre of wool-working and wool-weaving, so it is not surprising that the embroidery, although done in silk, should be on a wool ground. The main piece is the draped dress, here called *hram*, worn for the seventh day of the marriage celebrations. It is about 4-4.5 m long by 1 m wide and may also be worn as a veil on special occasions.

Traditionally, the *hram* was of red wool and the embroidery, instead of being in horizontal bands as at Moknine or Kerkenna, formed a vertical panel down the front, which required the draping to be somewhat different. The old pieces (now very rare) are magnificent and much of their charm comes from their beautifully balanced asymmetry. On either side of the embroidered centre line there are larger or smaller squares, containing the round motif *gamra* – the moon, and tall motifs known as *'amud* – pillars. The latter is a peculiarity of the region; a tribute perhaps to the great amphitheatre. Scattered among these main geometric motifs are

A very unusual motif: a snake in a field of brightly coloured flowers couched and roughly embroidered silk on wool – veil from El Djem.

little camels, fish, birds, crescent moons, brides in the position of *jelwa* with their hands raised, tortoises and scorpions. These last are perhaps prophylactic, as is the case on certain skirts from Rajasthan, and may explain the crabs on the tunics from Raf-Raf; since in Arabic the worlds for crab and scorpion are the same — *'aqrab.*

Embroidery on a woollen veil from El Djem, principally worked in appliquéd cord. The free-standing circles are pearl buttons, perhaps, representing brides, their hands raised for the jelwa and the sun, or full moon.

The embroidery was done in brilliantly coloured silks — bright yellow, orange, green, blue, purple with a very little gold, mostly in the simplest back or running stitches ; the edges of the *hram* are decorated with multi-coloured silk tassels. The belt — as always very important — was made of strands of matching silk from which hung felt balls embroidered with gold, called "pomegranates". There is an especially beautiful example of an old *hram* in the *C.A.T.P.* collection.

More recent *hrams* instead of being all red are parti-coloured red and black (in direct contradiction, incidentally, to the story about parti-coloured dresses reported in the section on Le Kef p.142) and the design, often pillars and moon alternating, radiates out from the central division, with hands, fish and so on in the interstices. As well as silk embroidery, a certain amount of applied silk cord is used, very discreetly in the earlier pieces. An especially splendid example, worked almost entirely in neutral colours on a red ground, is to be found in the Musée des Arts Africains et Océaniens in Paris. It has a strange combination of moons and what are perhaps *jelwa* figures, and elements of the pattern are heightened by mother-of-pearl buttons, making a particularly African effect.

The most modern ones, however, are often done entirely in gold cord and spangles and are very much less interesting.

Ksour Es-Saf

Smaller head-shawls are also worn at El Djem, but they generally come from Ksour Es-Saf, another great centre of wool-working – indeed the name may be a dialect rendering of "Castle of Wool". These shawls have the peculiarity of being embroidered by men and are often signed. The older ones are made of black wool and the embroidery consists of applied and couched – *tanbit* – cord, not gold, but in quite neutral colours with touches of red and blue. They generally have a large round moon motif and then geometric designs – stylized combs, jewels, etc, rather than the fish and birds beloved of the women. Some of the motifs do, however, suggest the somewhat outer-space-like creatures, which also crop up on the Gabès embroideries. Modern ones tend to be in gold thread with a little colour on black velvet. This should be quite effective, but for some reason is often tawdry, probably on account of the quality of the gold and also the less careful workmanship.

Embroidery motif from a woollen veil from El Djem – perhaps brides and tree of life.

Sitt Enfisa

> *Oh my lady, oh Saint,*
> *Shower your blessings on me!*
> *Oh my lady, by the head of your son*
> *And by your husband and his fair posterity!*
> *You, for whom the mountains grew light,*
> *You, for whom the very seas made way!*

*   *   *

The nearby town of Djebeniana is famous for its fine weaving and it is claimed that the techniques were invented and handed down by a local saint, Sitt Enfisa, who is said to have come from Arabia "a long, long time ago". Offerings are made to Sitt Enfisa and she is invoked before a complicated piece of work is begun. Traditionally, when a girl began to weave at the age of about twelve, her family would offer a meat couscous with some dates to both the saint and her father, Sidi Bou Sh'aq, another marabout. It was also customary to bury a number of eggs. The family would spend the night near the tomb of Sitt Enfisa and if in the morning the girl succeeded in finding the eggs, it was thought that the saint had "accepted" her and she would become a good weaver. If she failed, it was a very poor omen for her apprenticeship.

GABÈS AND THE SOUTH

Gabès, the last major town of the Tunisian South existed already before the Romans, who called it Tacapa. It seems to have been abandoned and was re-founded in the 7th century by Sidi Boulbaba, the Prophet's barber, in whose mosque there were, facing the mihrab, many ex-votos, including pieces of weaving and embroidery, besides the floor carpets offered by the faithful.

*   *   *

Your beauty pleases me – my eyes have seen
*   nothing to compare with you.*
Your sash swathes your body, it goes round
*   sixteen times.*
It is a sash with tassels, it wraps gently about
*   you and reaches the ground.*
It is so pretty with its many colours, it is a new
*   chessboard with its contrasting squares.*

I like it thus – white, and red with cochineal; it
*   appears to float softly*
On your indigo dress. It sways about my friend
*   with the amorous eyes.*
It reaches the calf; it has many different shades
*   and pompoms.*
This is the sash worn by my friend with the dark
eyes, and the wool seems to weigh more than
*   200 pounds.*

*   *   *

Gabès is in an area where weaving is definitely more important than needlework as means of decoration, but nevertheless the region has a type of embroidery on wool, peculiar to itself, which can really only be paralleled in the Kebili and, perhaps, at El Djem.

The most striking pieces are the smallish (generally about 1 m square) head or shoulder coverings, principally from the Chenini district. They are woven and then dyed with rows of tie-dye circles. This form of decoration, which has been found from both Pharaonic and Coptic Egypt, occurs sporadically in North Africa, always on wool – there are quite elaborate examples from Libya and

Wool on wool embroidery over tie-dye from Gabès. Probably a 'shoulder piece', early-mid 20th century

Morocco — and it is associated with the Berber regions; indeed, in French, this form of tie-dye is known as "Berber batik". Thread is tied round grains of wheat to make the resist-dyed pattern — in Tunisia usually simply rows of dots. Some of the *bahnug* (as these pieces are called, or, in the case of little girls' shawls, *mendila*), have just a small line of geometric embroidery in wool along their upper edge; this work is normally done by men. There are others, surely worked by women, which have much more complicated designs, not unlike those made in silk by the Jewish women of the oasis, or the splendid pieces from El Djem. Done as a rule in warm colours — reds, yellows, oranges and white predominating — over the tie-dye, favourite motifs included birds, but usually cocks rather than doves or peacocks; the hand, sometimes with what would seem to be an eye on the palm; the *gamra*, or moon; crosses; strange creatures which could be butterflies — or perhaps fish; elongated motifs which might be palm-trees, or even people stylized out of all recognition; lines of what look like attempts at writing — the signature of the maker? expressions of good luck?

This type of embroidery is completely different from that of the towns. To begin with, both in the choice of colours and in the way of stylizing motifs, it suggests Africa rather than the Mediterranean.

Secondly, although technically very rustic — the large stitches, basically running stitches arranged in lines, circles, zigzags, etc — these pieces have a bold effectiveness which the urban pieces sometimes lack. Thirdly, like the shawls and draped dresses from El Djem, they are very personal. The stylization of the figures is not like the almost official formality of, say, the tulip in Turkish art, but something more naive, certainly more primitive.

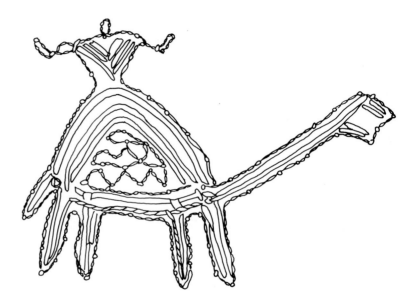

Camel bearing a bride in the position of jelwa, *appliqué and rough embroidery on wool – Gabès.*

Unfortunately, I know much less about this area and have seen far fewer examples than I would have wished, but these wool embroideries seem similar in range of motifs to those which the Jewish women of the region used to work in silk on the geometrically woven *melhafa* and *'ajar*, apparently for a Muslim clientèle. Another analogous type of embroidery, very rich, especially prized and much imitated, was that of the black women of Méthouia – and so it is possible that the patterns were originally introduced into the region from south of the Sahara.

The women of the Gabès oasis also provide several pieces of "local dress" to other nearby towns – for example the small square shawls, not unlike those already described, but embroidered in bright colours on a red ground, with an edge of many coloured pompoms for the women of Médenine; or the red embroidered head-covering with its red and green pompoms, worn with the marvellously antique-looking scarlet and white draperies at Hadège in the Matmata on the wedding night.

Gabès is also famous for its lace, in particular its sleeves embroidered on net and its crochet plastrons, which are supplied to the whole region and even further afield. Here, it was the Jewish women of El Hamma who were considered to produce the finest work.

It is perhaps worth mentioning that the splendid weaving of this area (and indeed all the south) often looks like embroidery – white on dark red or dark blue – and has some of the usual patterns, fish, hands, etc, but it is in fact never done with a needle. As might be expected, the range of patterns is different from that of urban embroideries, with geometric motifs resembling the local tattoo marks and pottery decorations, as well as the kelim patterns – stylized combs, pieces of jewellery and so on. There are even faintly anthropomorphic figures reminiscent of Tanit and in one of the villages of the Matmata there is a pattern called *gad Zazia* – beautiful Djazia – after the heroine of the folk-epic of the Beni Hilal. These pieces are quite frequently offered for sale and it is reasonably true that white was worn before marriage, red after and dark blue in old age, although this, obviously, can vary from village to village and region. A girl would traditionally try to bring as many pieces as she could with her as her dowry, preferably enough to last her whole lifetime, since once she had children there would be little time for weaving herself pretty things.

"Beautiful Djazia" – a motif found not only on textiles, but also on pottery and tattoos – Gabès and the southern oases.

HAMMAMET

Hammamet – the name means "Baths" or "Hot Springs" – is in the rich agricultural area known as Cap Bon and stands on one of the most beautiful bays in Tunisia. In Roman times there was a town nearby and now Hammamet is the centre of one of the country's largest tourist development areas. Its very charming and pictures-que kasbah, although inhabited, is largely geared to tourism, with numerous shops selling souvenirs, local arts and crafts. In view of this, it is surprising that Hammamet is a highly conservative town and has maintained, at least in part, a very elaborate and varied local costume.

Embroidery on wool

The basic dress, which used also to be worn at Nabeul, is a sleeveless tunic – *jebba* – slightly flared at the bottom, made of a very pleasant loosely woven black wool gauze, which varies in consistency and may be as light as a heavy butter muslin. Tradi-tionally, the women prepared every stage of this cloth themselves, except the shearing and the weaving. Dyeing, rather surprisingly, was a female task and the black was obtained from pomegranate rinds boiled with blueing. The knee-length tunic was worn over a white chemise with the usual wide detachable embroidered net sleeves (see Lace p.82) and white Victorian-looking pantaloons which just showed at the hem, leaving the lower leg bare.

More elaborate versions of this served for ceremonial occa-sions. Early this century, the tunic would be half black and half red (analogous tunics at Monastir were red and blue) and the type is still sometimes worn for the second day of the marriage. This tunic has a horseshoe-shaped neck, open almost to the waist, and bound by a great plait of passementerie, each strand being made up of numerous very thin gilded wires, bound at intervals with turquoise, blue or violet silk. The shoulders have small stiff "wings", again made of passementerie braid, backed as a rule on red or orange silk. The passementerie, like that on many of the *farmla*, or short bolero jackets, the Raf-Raf tunics, and so on, was the province of specialists, although some women made it simply for their own use at home. The techniques involved are elaborate, but hardly qualify as embroidery.

Child's dress, embroidered on black wool gauze and accompanying blouse with wide embroidered net sleeves. Hammamet, first half of the 20th century.

The third development of this dress, which is still worn on ceremonial occasions today, is again all black. It has the same neck and "wings" as the parti-coloured version, and is called *jebba matruza*. The difference is that it is embroidered with gold, sometimes just on the bottom half of the skirt, or else all the way up. It is finished off with quite elaborate bands of embroidery at the bottom and around the neck, often forming a kind of garland. The pattern over the body of the tunic is almost invariably flowers or stars, sometimes stylized down to four spots or squares, and arranged in regular rows. They are couched using gold sequins or canetille. Sometimes, for a yet richer effect, the space between the flowers is filled in with rows of vaguely star-shaped dots made of the flat gilded silver thread called *tal*, which is passed back and forth through the loose weave of the cloth. A similar technique occurs on Turkish towels.

As can easily be imagined, the effect of these tunics is both splendid and pretty. They are the only ones that I have ever seen that are made in a small version for little girls.

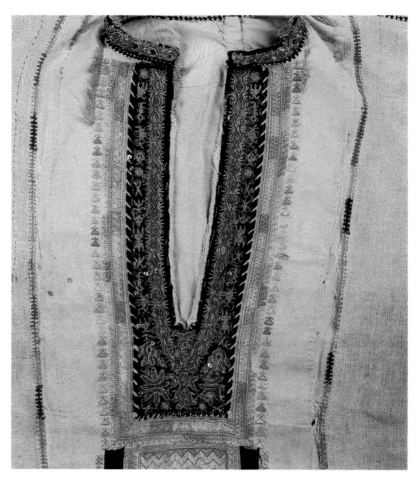

Tunic from Hammamet, showing the different types of linen of which it is made and the black and gold work. Note the small figures, perhaps 'brides' outlining the plastron. Late 19th century

Embroidery on linen or cotton

Another completely different type of embroidery done by the women of Hammamet is that found on the simple rectangular tunic – *qmejja* – worn under several of the ceremonial costumes which will be discussed later. This tunic is of the very ancient type, described for Mahdia and Moknine – a single strip of material folded in half with a hole for the head, a slit down the breast and two side seams. The oldest ones are of hand-woven linen – *souria*, probably from Syria – the later ones of cotton. Silk ribbons are sewn down it vertically. One in my possession, perhaps seventy-five to a hundred years old, is entirely made of very narrow strips of linen (not all the same) joined with lines of multicoloured embroidery in a kind of feather stitching – and this arrangement is typical of the older pieces.

The important embroidery, however, is on the central band,

since this is what shows under the slightly opened ceremonial caftan. In the more recent pieces, this is fairly solid gold work – since the craft of the embroideress has become less prized than sheer weight of metal. The older pieces have a neckband and small plastron made of blackwork with good-luck motifs in gilt and sometimes silver, the fish and the hand typically predominating. Sometimes the entire strip – approximately 1.20 m x 15-25 cm – is surrounded by a shoal of gilt fish. Below this plastron come two smallish panels, approximately 10 cm across and 15 cm long, separated and framed by long stripes of black work, done largely in forms of Gobelin stitch, especially upright and plaited, which give a very elegant effect.

It has been suggested that this black work in Tunisia is another Andalusian survival. Indeed, it was the great Spanish speciality in the Renaissance (when the aristocracy wore little except black) which soon spread through Europe; Catherine of Aragon, Henry VIII's first wife, is traditionally credited with introducing it into England. The influx of refugees in 1609-10 would therefore have occurred at exactly the right moment to carry it into North Africa.

Incidentally Lemta (ancient Leptis Minor) had a distinctive tunic, generally commissioned from the embroideresses of Moknine, who made a heavy decoration of black work, which was then re-embroidered with gold at home.

The small panels are charming and, as far as I know, a peculiarity of Hammamet not found elsewhere in Cap Bon. The more recent ones are very brightly coloured, the older ones were always less strident and have faded to beautiful soft shades of apricot/pink/ mauve/brown, reminiscent of the rural embroideries of Chéch-aouen in Morocco. The little panels suggest samplers with lines of different motifs: triangles, stars, wavy lines – "drunkard's step", very formal flowers – "jasmine", and sometimes a line of good-luck symbols, especially camels, although fish are not unknown, and the hand is generally found somewhere, so stylized as to be almost unrecognisable. The camel so far from the desert is less surprising than one might think, for in this region it is still the animal most commonly used for ploughing and, perhaps more relevantly, it served all over the Sfax area and even further North to carry the bride to the house of her groom in an elaborately decorated litter. There are also little satin stitch triangles with a few stitches above vaguely suggesting head and hands, which may be "brides".

It is clear, however, that the motifs have become so stylized that even the embroideresses are not really aware of what they are – on one pieces in my possession the "brides" are on their heads and the camels balance on their humps with four legs in the air.

The stitches used are mostly variants of satin, back, stem, brick and occasionally a rather approximate attempt at Algerian star stitch. The effect is charming, the formality of the black work providing an admirable contrast to the rustic "samplers". It would be easy to copy perhaps even for the traditional use down the front of a blouse or dress.

Detail showing black work and 'sample' panel from a Hammamet tunic. Note that in this case the 'sampler' with its little camels, 'Hands of Fatima' etc, is upside down

Gold embroidery

The other embroidery techniques used in Hammamet all concern gold embroidery of the usual kind and so will be dealt with quickly. There are three main pieces of clothing involved.

One of the most splendid costumes of Tunisia is the Hammamet golden marriage tunic – *el-kiswa el-kebira* or great veil – worn on the day of *jelwa*. It is put on over the linen tunic described above, a short gold-embroidered bolero jacket and a purple caftan – (see below).

In the past this tunic, which evolved from the archaic type preserved at Mahdia was made of alternating vertical bands (typically 14) of woven silk ribbon and gold-embroidered silk. It was common to many Tunisian cities along the coast, but the base colours varied and each town tended to have its own preference:

Hammamet – orange

Menzel Temime – red

Monastir – yellow or pale blue (apparently where the fashion originated)

Raf-Raf – purple

Soliman – grey blue

Sousse – dark green or black.

The gold work was originally rather delicate, mostly in the flat kind of thread, *tal*, and the designs were floral scrolls with occasional hands and fish, showing a great deal of background. Gradually, however, with the passage of time (and perhaps increased prosperity) there developed the wish to show off more and more gold, with the result that the tunics became so heavily worked that the ground no longer showed and became quite rigid – like the front panel of the Moknine tunic. The bride who wears one has to be careful not to scratch herself, particularly since her face is also covered with a veil stiff with gold. The effect is extraordinarily rich and brilliant, but suggests, to me at least, armour rather than clothing and is not in fact very beautiful.

Interestingly enough, this dress is analogous to a 10th-century Fatimid one found at Fostat in Egypt. Certain items of Tunisian costume may therefore have, as the folk tradition claims, a very long genealogy.

The second garment is a knee-length caftan worn outside on the seventh day of the marriage – it was put under the tunic on the day of *jelwa*. As a rule it is of purple velvet couched with gold. Worn open down the front to show the embroidery on the tunic below, it is held by a splendid matching belt ritually put on that day. The designs on the skirts of the caftan are flowery scrolls with fish and birds, developing up and out from the bottom front corners. On the short bell-shaped sleeves there is invariably a Hand of Fatima flanked by two fish. Under these sleeves the bride wears two or three sets of the extremely wide, light, detachable ones so common in Tunisian costume. The outer ones are white silk embroidered with gold and huge sequins, which hang down to the edge of the caftan, while the inner ones are of white embroidered lace. The headdress is a small pill-box with an aigrette in front and a tassel at the side – like the caftan it is very clearly of Turkish origin. Embroidered in gold and stiffened with layers of cardboard, these are generally made by saddlers. The rest of the embroidery was traditionally a Jewish speciality and the caftan is further enriched by gold passementerie, including twelve huge decorative buttons down the side of the neck opening, each with a coral bead in the centre. These buttons, still made and used, though usually without the bead, are known as "mallow flower" from their shape. The whole costume is a particularly attractive one.

The third major piece of clothing is a black wool gauze robe with short orange silk sleeves, shaped like the caftan and similarly embroidered, called *kadrun*, which was worn for ceremonial occasions. There were also the gold-embroidered sleeveless jackets, *farmla*, and a range of headdresses, *qufiya*, which have been mentioned briefly elsewhere.

It should not be forgotten that there are all kinds of local variants, which unfortunately cannot be discussed here. That of Menzel Temime, for example, suggests a page boy in a Persian miniature and makes an extraordinary contrast with the draped dress of everyday — as of course these wedding clothes are intended to do.

The following description is part of a list of the innovations introduced into the court at Baghdad by Zubeida, the wife of Harun al-Rashid, and it comes from a 10th-century historical work, *The Meadows of Gold and Mines of Precious Stones* by Masudi:

"Zubeida, noticing her son's marked taste for these eunuchs and the ascendance they were gaining over him, chose young girls remarkable for the elegance of their figures and the charm of their faces. She had them wear turbans and gave them clothes woven and embroidered in the royal factories, and had them fix their hair with love-locks and draw it back at the nape of the neck after the fashion of young men. She dressed them in close-fitting wide-sleeved robes called *qaba* and wide belts which showed off their waists and their curves. Then she sent them to her son. Amin, as they filed into his presence, was enchanted. He was captivated by their looks and appeared with them in public. It was then that the fashion for having young slave girls with short hair, wearing *qaba* and belts, became established at all levels of society. They were called 'page girls'."

Vol I, translated by Paul Lunde and Caroline Stone

Embroideresses and techniques

Although many of the most sumptuous pieces, in particular the caftan and the gold marriage tunic, are no longer made, Hammamet families often still have an embroidery frame – *gorgaf* – on which they work sleeves, short jackets and their wool or linen tunics in their spare time. A number of items are also produced for the Office de l'Artisanat, which allots piece-work to several hundred embroideresses, for whom it is an agreeable way of increasing the family income. The objects made are intended largely for sale to tourists and to some extent for export and are mostly tablecloths, household linen, cushion covers, children's clothes and so on, worked principally in the Nabeul manner, which has spread widely in the wake of official training courses, rather as Fez embroidery has done in Morocco.

Traditionally, the clothes were made up first, usually rather clumsily, and embroidered afterwards; but first the design would be drawn free-hand on the cloth by a *rassama*, a professional who was not necessarily an embroideress. It would take her the better part of ten days or a fortnight (remembering that she would be working in her spare time) to draw out the pattern on a *kadrun* or robe. The actual embroidery would then be done at home – often by a young girl for her dowry – or, in the case of the richest families and the most complicated pieces, by a professional embroideress, very often Jewish. A sampler or *tanquila* showing the traditional designs, particularly those for embroidery on linen was, in the past, part of the equipment of many Hammamet households. Sadly, today these have frequently been offered for sale, suggesting that they are no longer needed.

Although Hammamet is relatively traditional, these very splendid costumes are undoubtedly disappearing. There are all sorts of reasons. Women are no longer uneducated, as they were thirty years ago, and consequently have more possibilities and interests and less time to devote to the embroidery frame. Also, fashions change and many girls now want to be married in the "modern" Tunis style.

Furthermore, there is the question of economics. A combination of the restrictions on imports after 1962 and the departure of a good number of Jewish families made fine quality metal thread and other necessary items almost unobtainable. In addition the prices of silver and gold have risen steeply. The result has of necessity been the use of inferior materials for making these items of clothing, which therefore no longer have an intrinsic value as well as that of craftsmanship. The fact that the resale value may not be high discourages women from keeping their "nest-egg" in this form –

especially since there are now so many other options, as well as so many other things to buy. The prices of the articles themselves are also undoubtedly a factor, although perhaps not so much as one would think in view of the prices of the Tunis-style dresses now favoured. Samira Sethom, in her article of 1968 gives £16 as the price of a cotton tunic, £50-£75 for a *jebba* and £400 for a gold marriage tunic. One could multiply roughly by 4 to get the cost of commissioning these pieces today – yet the price they would command second-hand in 1983 would only be between 50 per cent and 100 per cent of the 1968 price – and the seller would only get a fraction of it, at best around 25 per cent.

All in all, it is sad but hardly surprising that these very splendid clothes, worn only a few times in a woman's life, should no longer be made and that there should be an increasing tendency to hire them for the marriage day. The idea of lending wedding clothes for the *baraka* – blessing – seems less strong in Hammamet than in Bizerte and up towards the Algerian border, but this is only an impression of mine and I may well be wrong.

LE KEF AND THE WEST

The position of Le Kef justifies its name of "The Rock", but it is also known as Chikka Benar from the Latin Sicca Veneris. It has a famous temple dedicated to the Great Goddess, whom the Romans identified with Venus, and the ritual prostitution practised there allegedly shocked the more puritanical of the colonials. Said to have been evangelized by Saint Augustine, the town become a great centre of monasticism. Under Islam, it became (and still is) equally famous for its marabouts – in the 19th century there were 49 *zaouias* in a population of 3,000 people.

Le Kef and the region around it is interesting and different from the coast, partly because of the definite Algerian influence and partly because the incursions of the Beni Hilal, as the historian Ibn Khaldun tells us, led to the indigenous Berbers, who were sedentary agriculturalists with perhaps a last remnant of classical city culture, becoming nomads, or at least transhumant, and adopting the language, customs and religion of their Muslim conquerors. It was not until the coming of the Turks that the region was once more properly urbanized.

The embroidery

Le Kef and Western Tunisia have no particular local tradition of embroidery, unless, which is perfectly possible, some small pockets exist of which I am not aware, and, like Bizerte, tended to commission or imitate gold embroidery from the capital. The local costume does have an interesting peculiarity in that the wedding clothes are in the sacred colours traditionally associated with the marabouts – red and green. It is a combination which no-one visiting Tunisia can fail to notice – on the columns in the souk in Tunis, around the doorways of the saints' shrines, striping the banners at festivals. These, or very similar colours, have a special meaning in many countries – turquoise and orange in Ancient Egypt, for example, or red and white combined and green in Mediaeval England. At Le Kef, the bride wears a red and green parti-coloured velvet tunic decorated with gold passementerie on the first day of the wedding. It has under it a chemise with particularly pretty blue and white check sleeves, slightly reminiscent of the "tattooed" robes of Raf-Raf. On the seventh day, she puts on the draped dress, which is the real costume of the region, a green one over a red one, thus maintaining the colour schemes. In the past, she might also have worn a third yellow one underneath. With this, of course, she wears a belt made of red, yellow and green silk cords embroidered together with silver thread by a technique called "strangled" because the stitches are drawn so tight. Recently, there has been a tendency to use orange rather than a true red.

Parti-coloured robes

The whole question of parti-coloured robes, so reminiscent of those of the European Middle Ages, is fascinating and although it is not possible to go into the question in detail here, it does seem worth giving a list of some of the main colour schemes, at least in Tunisia. In fact, they are known all over North Africa. A. Rubens mentions them in Tripoli last century as being a peculiarity of the Jewish community, but it seems to me more likely that it was a style that had once been general, but which by that date the Jews alone had preserved. It is often claimed that the fashion came from Andalusia – certainly it existed there, for various miniatures and the four sheikhs in parti-coloured robes painted on the ceiling of the Alhambra in Granada prove it. But, on the other hand, it seems to have struck a responsive chord in the Berber community and it is possible that the Spanish immigrants simply reinforced some tradition or superstition which they already had. Certainly it is deep-rooted. Mathea Gaudry writing in the 1960s about Algeria gives the following revealing anecdote:

"A woman of the tribe of Khementa at Aflou, having gone into the tent of one of her relatives, the ex-caid (chief) Benhamou, wearing a draped dress made in two colours after the ancient now-abandoned manner, the old man told her to leave at once, saying that such clothes were liable to bring down misfortunes on the live-stock. An abandoned tradition constitutes a danger on no account to be awakened."

Parti-coloured clothing exists in many places in North Africa and especially in Tunisia, so here is a list of the principal places where it is found, with colour schemes:

El Djem : red/black "veil", the two halves joined with
                embroidery
Hammamet : red/black (also quardanine)
Le Kef : red/green (also Beni Khaled, Feriana, Gafsa,
                Kerkenna)

La Kesra : blue/green
Ksar Hellal : green velvet jacket with red sleeves
Moknine : green velvet jacket with violet sleeves
             red/blue *hellala* (draped dress)
Monastir : red/blue
Raf-Raf : dark blue/black wool (early 20th century)
             purple/pink silk (mid-20th century)
Sfax : red/yellow, red/green, red/blue (19th century)
        pink/blue (20th century), sometimes made reversible
        – pink side out for the wedding, blue side out for the
        bride's first two outings after the marriage.
Sousse : dark blue/black, brown/black, dark blue/brown
            (19th century)
Tunis : emerald/purplish-red hip-length tunic (early 19th
            century)

MAHDIA

The first stone of Mahdia al-Hilalein — "Mahdia of the Two Crescent Moons" — so-named for its two bays, was laid by the schismatic Obeid Allah al-Mahdi, the founder of the Fatimid dynasty. Originally conceived as a fortress, for the Mahdi was hated by many for his fanaticism, Mahdia was a place of refuge during the incursions of the tribes of the Beni Hilal. The inhabitants lived by fishing, trade and above all piracy, against Sicily and Italy in particular. This led to reprisals, first in AD 1088, and then between 1148 and 1160 when it was occupied by Roger of Sicily. Sicily was at this date still very closely linked culturally with the Islamic world and a desire to protect her export trade was no doubt added to the wish to end the menace of coastal raids. The following description of Norman Sicily comes from *The Travels of Ibn Jubayr*, who visited the island while making the pilgrimage to Mecca from his home in Andalusia:

> "The handmaidens in his (King William) palace are all Muslims. One of the strangest things told us by this servant, Yahya ibn Fityan the Embroiderer, who embroidered in gold the king's clothes, was that the Frankish Christian women who came to his palace became Muslims, converted by these hand-maidens....
>
> "The Christian women of this city (Palermo) follow the fashion of the Muslim women, are fluent of speech, wrap their cloaks about them, and are veiled. They go forth on this Feast Day (Christmas) dressed in robes of gold-embroidered silk, wrapped in elegant cloaks, concealed by coloured veils, and shod with gilt slippers...bearing all the adornments of Muslim women, including jewellery, henna on the fingers and perfumes."

To return to Mahdia, in 1390 the French and the Genoese tried to take it (Froissart describes the expedition) and in 1549, the Turkish corsair Dragut (who at one stage in his long career was captured by the Genoese off Corsica and ransomed in exchange for the right to build a sea-castle at Tabarka near the Algerian border and fish coral there) succeeded. In 1550, the town was taken by the Spaniards, who, on their departure four years later, blew up many of the principal buildings, including the mosque of Obeid Allah, which is now restored.

Mahdia today is a quiet town – the tourist centre is slightly away from it down the coast – but it is still important for its crafts, in particular its weaving, which, together with the beautiful faces of the locals and their clean clothes, were already being praised by al-Idrisi in the 12th century. Mahdia is also known, but to a lesser extent, for its gold embroidery.

The embroideries

Although Mahdia has been an urban centre for a thousand years, it is quite firmly an area where draped rather than cut and sewn clothes were traditionally worn.

Its most characteristic piece of clothing is, however, a tunic – essentially the *tunica recta* – which can be paralleled exactly with those worn by figures in certain of the palaeo-Christian mosaics now in the Musée du Bardo at Tunis. Similar tunics can also be seen in Byzantine mosaics and those at Ravenna, and the arrangement of the embroidered rectangle on the breast and vertical bands suggest on the one hand the figures on the Coptic tapestry of the Orantes (Egypt, Akmim 7th century) and on the other the dresses of modern Jordan, Syria and Palestine.

The Mahdia tunic was originally linen, but is now cotton, and it is either about 1 m wide and 1.10 m long, or else somewhat shorter for everyday wear. There is no shoulder seam, but in order to make up the width, when the cloth is woven on a narrow loom, a panel is added under the arm-hole sewn in with decorative red and green embroidery in one of the zig-zag stitches. The front is stitched low on the breast and there is a plastron of solid black embroidery – *triza kahla* – of the kind used for the front of many of the coifs – *qufiya* – and in white or natural on men's robes. These vertical rows of stitches, for example bands of slanted satin stitch or broad stem stitch, alternating with basket stitch or double back stitch, with, as an outer border, curly Rhodian stitch, is extraordinarily elegant and effective. Below the slit there is a similar panel of solid horizontal rows from which descend lines of black work with white between to meet another solid horizontal panel at the hem. The descending rows may be in quite a variety of line stitches, including ones not found elsewhere – it will be noticed that Tunisia in general uses a relatively restricted repertoire – although chain and knotted stiches are not common. The designs of these lines, which are always geometric, vary from piece to piece, but are very strongly reminiscent of the tattoo patterns of the women of the area.

This black and white central panel is flanked by broad silk ribbons, two on each side, which continue down the back. They are like those of Moknine, but in dark indigo blue and pomegranate red with thin patterns in yellow, red and green running down them. The tunic is finished off at the bottom and the armholes with a row of soft silk tassels in red and green, and a similar pompom decorates the bottom of the front opening in such a way that it shows from under the other clothes worn on top.

In the past, a girl would make twenty or thirty of those tunics for her trousseau. On the Day of Henna it was customary to wear seven of them one on top of the other, and they would also be worn for the three or four days before the marriage and the three days afterwards. The tunic would, of course, be worn for the *jelwa* with, over it, a very large and long sleeveless jacket solidly couched in gold and silver with bold flowered scroll designs. The similarity of this garment to a chasuble has often been remarked on.

Traditionally on the seventh day, the Day of the Belt, the bride put on the draped dress which she would wear for the rest of her life. On this particular occasion the draped dress was of black wool made in two sections, one 3 m and one 2.5 m long, embroidered with vertical lines of red, white and green in designs very similar to the black ones on the tunic. These lengths of wool were edged with a broad band of gold braid interspersed with more coloured embroidery, and finished with the soft tassels of red and green silk. Worn over an almond green velvet jacket embroidered with vertical bands of gold flowers and left open to show the black embroidery on the plastron, the effect was splendid in a very different way from the carapaces of gold from Nabeul or Sousse, and somehow suggest the nomad more than the urban fashions.

Mahdia tunic, early 20th century. These are still made and were traditionally used for everyday wear under the draped dress of the region

The tunics we have described are still worn today, although the rest of the wedding costume has changed in response to modern fashion. For everyday use, they are short and only the black plastron with its pompom is visible under the draped dress. They are even worn by widows, who remove, however, the silk tassels as a sign of mourning.

MOKNINE

Moknine is a small town in the Sahel, not very interesting to look at, which has long had a notable Jewish community, allegedly descended from those expelled from Mahdia by the Spaniards in the 16th century. They were the jewellers and produced the particularly fine pieces of filigree and enamel for which the area is famed. They also made very high quality gold thread and sequins, which were much in demand, and the women were well-known as embroideresses.

Gold-embroidered marriage tunics

The costume of Moknine was largely derived from that of Mahdia and the most striking item was the splendid tunic or *qmejja*. Basically a rectangle of the most ordinary cotton cloth called *malti* (perhaps from Malta), and there are even examples worked on sugar sacks, the tunic is shapeless, sleeveless and roughly sewn together by machine. It is about 1 m long and down the front there is a panel some 25-30 cm wide of solid gold embroidery. The upper part, normally not seen because of the jewellery, has a square neck and is open down the breast. It is usually embroidered with wiggly vertical lines suggesting snakes, although the resemblance may be fortuitous, for snakes are more feared than venerated in Tunisia and are not often represented except on earrings from the islands and some country districts. The lower part is worked in horizontal registers of very bold motifs: bosses suggesting the sun and not dissimilar to those on the black Raf-Raf marriage tunics; square or diamond-shaped "mazes"; lines of fish; doves; the Hand of Fatima, separated from each other by lines, again usually wavy, suggesting water. The embroidery is almost entirely worked in flat gilt silver thread couched over thick cotton – almost cord – to give enormous solidity and relief, suggesting metal-work rather than cloth. Occasionally, a little fine gold thread is used as background couching to allow the motifs to stand out in yet greater relief. There are a very few touches of coloured silk, suggesting the enamels of the local jewellery, and their colours are repeated in the tassels of soft silk along the bottom and sometimes down the sides or in a horizontal row about halfway up. On either side of the central panel are sewn two broad silk ribbons, originally hand woven on a little loom, but later factory produced, one green decorated with red and the other red with green — colours with a maraboutic significance, as we have seen at Le Kef and elsewhere. A very similar tunic, but with a wider and longer gold panel, was worn for the day of putting on the belt — *tahzim*. Typically, the registers were divided into two by a line of silk tassels down the centre.

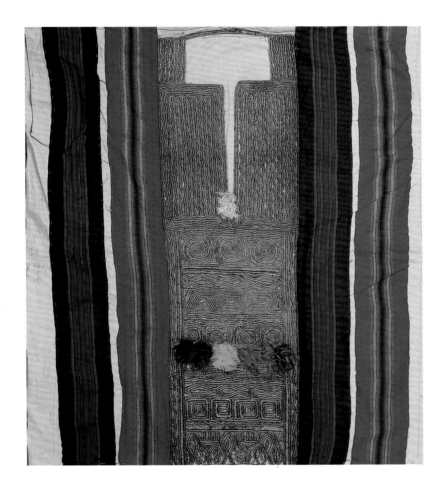

Wedding tunic from Moknine. Early 20th century

Hellala and the crescent moon

There is a particularly beautiful example of this type of work in the Moknine Museum not, however, on a tunic, but on a *hellala*. *Hellala* is the local name for the length of cloth worn all over rural Tunisia, draped and held by one or two fibulae and a belt. In this case the name is interesting because it comes from *hellal*, the word for the crescent-moon shaped brooches worn in that area, and non-literate folk-etymology derives both *hellala* and *hellal* from *hilal*, the classical Arabic for crescent moon. This in turn is connected with the Beni Hilal – the Tribe of the Crescent Moon – who came from Arabia to settle in North Africa in the 10th century, and whose loves and wars, related in the Romance of the Beni Hilal, constitute one of the great Arab folk-epics. The nearby town of Ksar Hellal – Castle of the Hellal – now principally known for its weaving and dyeing, is again said to take its name from the tribe. A last point concerning the crescent moon, which, with the star, is the outstanding symbol of Islam and one that is found everywhere and in every medium: it was already old in North Africa at the time of the Muslim conquests, as the Punic funerary monuments in the Bardo Museum bear witness.

Bride wearing a hellala and in the position of jelwa couched in gold on a hellala from Moknine worn on the 7th day of the marriage for the ceremony of "putting on the belt".

Lions and ladies

To return to the *hellala* in the Moknine Museum – it is of the red-brown pomegranate-dyed wool, which is one of the traditional colours of the region, the other being indigo blue; pieces which are half and half are very occasionally found. It has a band of embroidery of the kind described on the tunics, but in two parts, designed so as to meet when the draperies are fixed in place. The technique is that which has been described above, but a larger number of types of gold thread are used. The motifs include two representations of the bride, one on the day of *jelwa*, with her hands raised in the time-honoured attitude of prayer and very clearly wearing her gold embroidered tunic, the other on the 7th day – *tahzim* – wearing a belt. In the former, the girl stands beneath a kind of pediment, with "mazes" to her right and fish to her left; in the latter she is under an arch of, perhaps, palm fronds with pairs of bosses, fish and squares, one on either side.

*　　*　　*

Oh lion who advances roaring in the night
Are you not afraid lest Aisha strike you with her
bracelets?

– sing the Berber women as the bride is led in to her husband.

Gold couched lion from a marriage tunic from Moknine.

The counterparts of the brides are two lions – undoubtedly the symbol of the bridegroom. Common in Punic and Roman art, the lion, although it vanished nearly a century ago, still has an important place in Tunisian folk-lore. Stories of women married to lions abound and they are, not very surprisingly, a common image of manliness, strength, virility, throughout North Africa. It will be remembered that the followers of Abd al-Krim fighting for the liberation of Morocco were known as the "lions of the Rif".

Lions were also often represented standing on either side of a tree to which they might be chained (a very archaic motif) and on the lintels of doors, especially in the Cap Bon region as "protectors of the hearth". The lion is also a powerful maraboutic symbol, in particular among the Aissaoui.

Headdresses

The other main type of embroidery associated with Moknine is on the *qufiya*, or coif. The front part is in black work, like that on the Mahdia tunics, with the long silk tail embroidered with flat gold thread. When worn it is covered with an orange-red silk square worked in the same flat thread and similar in design to the reversible green-purple ones of Ksar Hellal. The edges of both types are elaborately fringed and decorated and the central motif is the moon, *gamra*, generally conceived as the old moon in the new moon's arms. It is often worked in Turkish open-work, a kind of single faggot stitch, which is known in Tunisia by the Turkish name *barmaqli* – nothing to do with the Barmacides, exterminated more than a thousand years before, but derived from a word for the fretted wooden window screens, called in Arabic *mashrabiya*.

NABEUL

The Classical Neapolis succeeded a Punic town of unknown name. It was famous for its pottery and for its garum — a kind of strong fish sauce, doubtless the Roman version of Patum Pepperium.

The present-day town is pleasant but not exceptionally interesting, although its Friday market is one of the best in the region.

Nabeul has always been a great centre of arts and crafts. Besides a very active production of pottery, it is well-known for its iron-work (the pretty curving window-grills which are such a charming feature of old Tunisian houses, for example) and its scent production. Much of the jasmine and orange-flower water offered for sale in the souk of Tunis comes from there and it is also exported — Tunisia, incidentally, was a great exporter of scent and cosmetics throughout the Middle Ages.

Modern embroidery

Another local craft is embroidery. The traditional white or pale blue on white geometric embroidery has been adapted to all sorts of other colour schemes worked on a variety of articles principally for sale to tourists. With the spread of women's magazines and printed pattern books, a number of extraneous elements have crept in, principally from Norway, which oddly enough has a rather similar embroidery style, with the result that one may find a tablecloth with reindeer instead of camels, or Christmas trees instead of cypresses and palms. On the other hand, the work, if a little monotonous when seen in large quantities, is always very competently done and the effect is pleasant. The Centre de l'Artisanat employs several hundred women working at home and not only has a very good selection of their work for sale, but also a small collection of antique pieces which is well worth seeing. For those in Nabeul without a great deal of time, the Artisanat is also most helpful in providing or arranging demonstrations of the various local crafts, including embroidery and weaving.

Traditional embroidery on linen and cotton

The women of Nabeul traditionally wore a black wool gauze dress – *jebba* – of the type described in the section on Hammamet, with the same elaborate neckline. Versions of this dress existed last century all along the coast from Bizerte to Sfax. At Nabeul the neck opening showed a gold-embroidered bolero jacket – *farmla* – with the lines of "mallow flower" buttons and, below, the plastron of the tunic. As elsewhere, this was originally linen, for which cotton came to be substituted, and orginally it was embroidered with the kind of black work described in the sections on Hammamet and Mahdia.

Neck of Nabeul tunic showing ribbon applique, the gold work known as barmaqli *and the white work said to have originated in the Balkans and now the standard local style. Early 20th century*

It is said, however, that about a hundred years ago, a Circassian woman introduced a different sort of embroidery into one of the great families, and soon it was being copied avidly. This type of work is essentially geometric, with occasional, very stylized, leafy scrolls, and runs in bands all down the central panel of the tunic. The stitch used is mainly satin stitch and the motifs are very much those which might be found on an early English sampler. The motifs may be picked out with a very little flat gilt thread – *tal* – and the Hand of Fatima at the bottom in the centre is very common. The embroidery thread may be pale blue rather than white – this is, more specifically, typical of the neighbouring village of Dar Chabane, famous for its stone-cutters, who carved many of the beautiful portals in the Medina of Tunis. Examples from Dar Chabane are rare for it was the custom of the women to keep their linen wedding tunic to be used as their shroud.

The Nabeul tunic is the usual type, a rectangle folded at the shoulders, and it is embroidered before the sides are sewn up. It is further decorated by a plastron of flat gold thread worked in the extraordinary mechanical-looking open-work called *barmaqli* (it is very hard to believe that it is done by hand) which is typical of the region, and twelve or so silk ribbons, usually pink and mauve, or other pastel colours, sewn vertically. It has the usual embroidered net sleeves – last century they would have been silk. Altogether the Nabeul tunics are among the prettiest and certainly the most delicate of the Tunisian embroideries. Some of the most appealing and successful of the modern embroidery has preserved this white or pale blue with touches of silver or gold.

The same type of embroidery was done on men's shirts, which also had wide sleeves, but gathered in at the wrist, and on the short narrow-sleeved white cloth jackets worn by young men with wide Turkish trousers for the ceremony of their engagement. These have completely disappeared from use.

Couched gold panel from the front of a Nabeul marriage robe.

Gold embroidery

The *jelwa* costume is an even more brilliant version of that described in the section on Hammamet. Here, however, the tunic – *dohla* – is almost ankle length. It has a central band of large, very stylized flowers within medallions, extraordinarily ecclesiastical-looking, while the rest of the highly rigid tunic is done in the *barmaqli* open-work, so that it looks like a golden grill. This tunic is also known as *jebba el-'ain fil-'ain* – the "tunic of the eye against the eye". This is perhaps because all the holes suggest eyes and hence are considered prophylactic against the evil eye, which, as we have said before, is always greatly feared.

Over the upper part of the tunic a very abbreviated bolero is worn embroidered with sequins in a fish-scale pattern; these were made by the saddlers of Tunis. Under the tunic there are wide-bottomed pantaloons of yellow satin embroidered all over with flat gold thread (again very bold designs) and, to allow some flexibility, matching detachable sleeves are fastened to the under tunic. As at Hammamet, the bride is (or was) veiled with cloth of gold under which she wears a coif – *qufiya* – with embroidered silk streamers which reach her waist. Gold embroidered slippers complete this literally dazzling dress.

As may easily be imagined, this costume is extremely uncomfortable and heavy. The clothes alone weigh many kilos (I have been told up to 20-25, but have never had an opportunity to weigh a complete set), to say nothing of the enormous quantity of jewellery. At one wedding which I had the honour to attend in this region in the mid-1960s, the bride, a healthy girl in her late teens, had difficulty standing up without help, her clothes were so stiff and heavy, and as she sat under the lights on the bridal throne, she was almost too brilliant to look at comfortably. Both of these effects are much valued.

As we have said before, an enormous accumulation of metal came to be more prized than grace or elegance and, by the same token, an armour-like stiffness is, or was until very recently, approved of. At Kaala Kbira, for example, the women called their tunics *cartonna* from the layers of card used to give them stiffness, with much the same technique as that described for the Hammamet headdresses.

RAF-RAF

Oh, regret for what is past!
Joy and all content!
Time has fled
And with him peacefulness.
Oh, lost world of Andalus –
Would that I might forget!

*   *   *

Raf-Raf is a small town on a headland south-east of Bizerte, traditionally famous for its muscat grapes and its embroideries. It constitutes one of those anomalies, not so very rare in North Africa: while such large important towns with long cultural traditions, as Bizerte, Sfax, Kairouan, Sousse, failed for various reasons to develop their own embroidery styles, Raf-Raf, with something over 10,000 inhabitants, not only has a lively and highly individual type of embroidery, but also particularly complicated forms of wedding costume, which have changed more than once this century. A number of the surrounding villages have less elaborate versions of the Raf-Raf style and it is remarkable that Raf-Raf should ever have been in a position to set, or indeed create, a fashion.

It is not known exactly when Raf-Raf, a pretty, picturesque town – the Romans knew it as Promontorium Pulchri – was founded. It is just north of a kind of lake open to the sea and fed by the Medjerda River. The nearby Ghar el Melh (once called Porto Farina) owes its existence to the famous 17th-century corsair, Ousta Murad, who, wishing to prevent the Christians from using the lake as anchorage (Charles V had used it as a base from which he attacked Tunis very successfully in 1541), built a fort and a port and encouraged Andalusians to come and live there. The neighbouring Galaat al-Andalus, the ancient Castra Cornelia, near Utica, was clearly also settled by them, and so perhaps was Raf-Raf. This, however, does not really solve the problem of the needlework, for Testour, further up the Medjerda, a town populated by refugees from Spain in 1609, genuinely has a number of Andalusian customs, from which it derives considerable cachet locally, but, as far as I have been able to discover, it has no particular embroidery tradition.

Plastron of an everyday Raf-Raf tunic, mid 20th century

Wool embroidery on cotton

The costume of Raf-Raf, and in particular its marriage costume, is complicated and both it and its evolution are admirably described in *C.T.F.T.* The most important item, however, in that it is both the most common and the most distinctive, is the tunic – the everyday version is called *suriya mabdu* – which occurs in a number of different forms. Basically, it is a rectangular garment, in the past sometimes made of linen, more recently cotton, and almost invariably striped vertically (occasionally one does find other patterns), red and white being by far the most usual combination. To this rectangle are added a pair of sleeves embroidered in coloured wool on net – *triz et-telli* – but without gold, as is described in the section on Lace.

The upper part of the armhole and the plastron are also decorated with very rich wool embroidery, essentially arranged in "ribbons" or bands. The colours are always brilliant and the range found in a bunch of anemones plus turquoise predominates. Over the wool embroidery, there will be sewn any number of sizes and types of sequins, canetille, gold and silver thread, flat or round, thick or thin, or flat tinsel, generally in red or green. I have seen robes with as many as seventeen different types of metal trimming. These are used to enhance the pattern and to make the whole effect as luminous as possible.

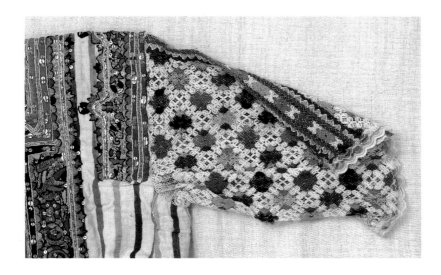

Sleeve of a Raf-Raf robe showing woollen embroidery on tulle. Mid 20th century

The outer band of the plastron and the inner one of the armhole generally consist of a ribbon of stylized flowers and lucky symbols worked on a silk ground, for which turquoise, violet and black are favourite colours. The outer edge of the band is often scalloped and there are similar embroidered scallops around the small stand-up collar; a flower grows at intervals. Inside the band there are usually lucky symbols alternating with leaves (especially what appear, appropriately, to be vine leaves) and flowers. Favourites are the peacock, the fish, the moon – full or crescent, with or without the star – a strange creature which seems to be a crab and, comparatively rarely, hands. On these tunics, I have never seen a human

Diving fish, possibly a dolphin holding a piece of red coral or the "horn which pierces the evil eye" in coloured wool with the touches of gold – Raf Raf.

figure, although they do occasionally appear on the jackets — pieces of clothing which often seem to carry the more unusual motifs — perhaps because they were worn underneath and so were more personal, being unseen?

Some tunics also have embroidery at the bottom, as a rule with a pyramid of flowers rising in the centre; oddly enough in view of the alleged Spanish origin, predominantly in black work.

These tunics were the everyday wear of Raf-Raf until very recently and, according to P. Ginestoux, girls would make several dozen of them for their trousseaux — which no doubt explains why so many are offered for sale, in spite of Raf-Raf being quite a small town. In fact, they are still made, both for local use and for sale to tourists. There has been a general tendency to increase the number of colours and general glitteriness over the decades, and some of the very recent pieces intended for sale to foreigners have lost their charm through the coarseness of the work and the very poor quality of the sequins, which produce a tawdry rather than opulent effect.

Jacques Revault, the great lover of Tunisia and expert on her arts and crafts, tells us that the women of Raf-Raf used to wear their tunics inside-out for everyday use so as not to spoil the embroidery doing housework. I have never seen this, but I have tried it myself and found it almost unbearably scratchy. Incidentally, in other areas of Tunisia, such as Sfax, wearing clothes inside out is a sign of mourning.

Techniques and stitches

Strip of Raf-Raf embroidery not yet made up, showing vine leaves, fish and other motifs

The Raf-Raf region, embroiders, like most of Tunisia, on a *gorgaf* or four-footed frame, which is generally associated with Turkey, and not on the Andalusian cushion. All the gold is couched — this type of embroidery is known as *tanbit* — while the wool is basically worked in satin stitch with a black stitch edging.

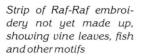

Tattooed tunics

A much grander version of the tunic described above is that known as *mwasma* – tattooed. It is worn on the 3rd day of the marriage as the over tunic, the *suriya mabdu* often being worn underneath. The *mwasma* is a relatively new development; it appears to have come into existence about 1925 as part of the general tendency towards elaboration.

In shape it is identical to the simpler tunic, although the neck may be cut square, and it is made out of a very ordinary cotton with a large red or orange check. Inside each square is embroidered a motif – essentially some form of flower or star – reminiscent of the tattoo patterns from which it takes its name. These are worked in colour, with or without a touch of gold – a single sequin in the centre of each flower, for example. The motifs at the back are often darker than those at the front, with black predominating.

Detail of Raf-Raf mwasma *tunic, showing the 'tattoos'*

The plastron is even more splendid and more heavily worked with gold than in the case of the ordinary tunics and the sleeves are, similarly, very rich (see Lace). The bottom of the robe has a band, again with much black and some colours and three pyramid-shaped motifs, mostly in gold, the tallest in the centre, representing as a rule a stylized vase of flowers, flanked by fish, peacocks, etc., with above it another stylized vase of flowers in black and colours. The band at the back is simpler with one "pyramid" in the middle. A very personal feature of these robes is the scattering of little good-luck symbols, done simply in black thread, here and there among the much more formal decoration. On one in my possession, these little doodles appear to be crabs, the precise significance of which I do not know.

Gold-embroidered marriage costumes

It is not possible to describe all the various costumes of Raf-Raf, but one or two more things should be mentioned. Most of the various wedding dresses are worn with the usual short jackets with "wings", which so much resemble the "clothes of light" of the bull-fighter. There are various shapes and kinds, all richly embroidered with gold, often on a ground of pink or purple silk. Surprisingly, they are often worn under the tunic and not on top as one would assume; this is particularly true of the ones without "wings". The heaviest type is known as *farmla* and the embroideries are often quite original, with friendly familiar chickens and even sheep wandering among the floral motifs and good luck signs.

Gold work is also very important on the other types of wedding dress and usually takes the form of an enormously heavy plastron often of passementerie — appliqués of gold braid, and so on, rather than real embroidery. This is particularly true of the older tunic for the third day of the marriage, which was made of the kind of loosely woven wool gauze described in the section on Hammamet. Sometimes parti-coloured, half blue, half black — a fashion which is said to

Section of the plastron of mwasma *tunic*

have originated in Spain and which has more or less survived to the present in many parts of North Africa – it has an enormous wreath of gilt curlicues round the neck and short bell-shaped sleeves, heavily worked with five-branched candlesticks and fish.

This marriage tunic was superseded at the beginning of the century by another parti-coloured one, this time in pink and purple silk. It again has a very elaborate plastron, this time shield-shaped and covered with the sort of work associated with orphreys.

The last type of embroidery is that found on the tunics used for the *jelwa* earlier this century and on some of the headscarves, including the type tied so as to form two wings – *taqrita m'asfra*, or "little bird scarf". The tunics are like those of Cap Bon, made out of alternating vertical ribbons of brocade and purple silk, the latter decorated with vertical bands of stylized flowers and arabesques couched in the flat gilt silver thread called *tal*. This flat silver thread, which gives a very particular effect, is found all over Tunisia – for example on the plastrons of the chemises at Nabeul or on the reversible green/purple head covers from Ksar Hellal – and is also characteristic of the towels from some areas of Turkey.

Origins

The relationship of Raf-Raf costume to that of Andalusia has been discussed at some length (see *C.T.F.T.*, which also gives bibliography) and apparently there are miniatures which show striped tunics with embroidered sleeves and plastrons. Interestingly, they seem to have been called in Spain, in the Middle Ages, *camisa margomada* – derived in turn from the Arabic *raqāma* – to embroider. The Spanish taste for black, which may have been more pronounced in the past, is still just visible on the bottoms of some tunics and in the needlework on the front of the Raf-Raf *qufiya* (coif), or headdress.

TOZEUR, NEFTA, KEBILI AND THE DJERID

Settled populations have worked the oases for millennia. The Romans knew Tozeur as Thusuros and Nefta as Aggasel Nepte, and both towns were on the Roman road which marked the southern boundary of the province of Africa. The area was heavily Christianized and was the site of particularly bloody battles between the Christian Berbers and the Muslim Arabs until Islam triumphed in the 8th century. The population did not, however, drift into nomadism as had happened in the West, presumably because it is essential that for agriculture an oasis should have incessant care. Throughout the Middle Ages, the region was known as Kastiliya, and in the 14th century Tozeur was said to have a population of 100,000, clearly an exaggeration, and her scholars were famous. From the 16th century she declined, thanks to the depredations of raids, cholera and so on.

The women of the South are excellent weavers, but there is traditionally little embroidery, although the Service de l'Artisanat has been encouraging it as a means for the women to earn extra money at home. This has been a great success, for the work is lighter and faster – and hence more remunerative – than weaving. The situation was not always thus, however, for Al-Tidjani, writing in the early 14th century, describes the Bab al-Manshur at Tozeur as follows:

> "Those of the inhabitants who exercise the profession of dyers come there to spread out garments of various colours, and embroidered stuffs. The eye of the visitor seems to see in front of him a rich flower-bed, where flowers of a thousand colours blossom on the edges of fresh and limpid streams."

This is by no means the case today.

*   *   *

On two things the Djerid survives
One is dead and one alive.
Local proverb

*   *   *

Even Nefta, so geared to textiles that it is divided into two parts according to the weaving done there – to the east, the Quarter of Silk and to the west, the Quarter of Wool – has very little in the way of embroidery. Like Tozeur, there is to be found hardly more than a few stitches along a border, or to join the two pieces of the *huli* (draped dress) or *melhafa* (veil, or rather head-covering – the same word was, incidentally, used in Andalusia).

Kebili has one interesting form of embroidery on the great black cotton *melhaf* (approximately 3.5 m × 1 m in size) worn by the women when they go out. It would seem to be a copy of the older silk veils of the Djerid which were woven on a narrow loom and had therefore to be joined lengthwise. The women of Nefzaoua used to decorate the seam with green and the women of Kebili embroider a green imitation seam to divide their *melhafa* into two. On either side they embroider geometric "ribbons" and motifs such as the moon, combs, etc in brilliantly coloured silks – white, pink, bright green, bright yellow, mauve, violet, scarlet – which stand out beautifully against the surrounding blackness.

*   *   *

Brother, today I saw my beloved,
She was wearing a draped dress from the Djerid.
She is the cause of all my grief, she will not yield
                                        to me.

Brother, I see her fresh blue tattoos
And love for her overwhelms me.
I go away depressed, without strength, my mouth
                                        dry.

*   *   *

There was one particular black family who was credited with introducing this style and bringing it to its greatest fineness, and when Jacques Revault wrote on the subject in 1960, there was still a member of the family working, Bent Abd El Ali. Both men and women in this family embroidered, and the *C.A.T.P.* in Tunis possesses two examples of the work of a woman of the family and her granddaughter.

TUNIS

"Tunis the white and scented bride of Africa"

Tunis was already known in Greek as "The White", a name by which she is still known poetically – *al-bayda*, or sometimes as *al-khadra* – "The Green". During the Classical period, power wavered between Tunis and Carthage, a few miles away across the lake, but the Arabs, arriving in the 7th century AD unequivocally made Tunis their base and Carthage fell into ruins. It was not until the 12th century that Tunis took the place of Kairouan as first city of what is now Tunisia, and enjoyed a period of great prosperity and intellectual vigour. In 1332, Ibn Khaldun, one of the greatest Arab historians, was born there. In the late 13th century, St Louis and the Crusaders made an attempt to take Tunis, but a peace was signed with the remarkably civilized clause that "the Christians living in Tunis could do so freely and have churches, and trade on the same terms as the Muslims." According to local tradition, St Louis converted to Islam on his death-bed and some say that he is in fact the saint Sidi Bou Said, whose shrine is venerated at the enchanting village of the same name just beyond Carthage.

Writing in the 16th century, Leo Africanus (born al-Hassan ibn Muhammad al-Wazzan) called Tunis "one of the most remarkable and splendid cities of Africa"; but at that date decline had already set in and shortly after, in 1534, Tunis was seized by the greatest of the Turkish corsairs, Khaireddine Barbarossa. The next year, Charles V elected to intervene – his victory is commemorated in a very fine and interesting series of tapestries hanging in the Alcazares Reales in Seville – and the Spaniards (Don John of Austria's name is remembered in this context) then played tug-of-war with the Turks for it until 1573. Tunis then came under the sway of Turkey – and various breakaway Turkish beys and deys – until 1881 when the French protectorate was established.

Tunis has a beautiful and unspoiled Medina, with many very splendid old palaces. Those interested in embroideries will find great quantities of all kinds, old and new, as they wander through the souks. Besides the obvious line of shops leading from the Porte de France to the Great Mosque, the Djemaa ez-Zitouna – Mosque of the Olive – there is the Souk et-Trouk (the Turkish souk, where once the tailors and embroiderers in the Turkish manner worked), the Souk el Berka (formerly the Slave Market), the Souk el Attarine

(Perfume Souk), which leads on the left, to the Cloth Souk, the Women's Souk and the Wool Souk – all places where embroidery may be found. Further on into the residential and working part of the Medina there are a good number of weavers' workshops, but the embroiderers tend to work at home and are not easily found. The famous saddle makers and gold embroiderers of the Souk es-Serrajine and the Souk es-Sekkajine have more or less vanished. A better place to look for embroidery workshops today is the Ville – around Rue Ibn Khaldun, or Rue Mohammed Ali, at Bab Khadra, or out on the first stretch of the road leading to the Bardo. The official Artisanat shop on Avenue Habib Bourguiba has, of course, a full selection of the best quality modern embroideries and a small collection of antique ones on display.

In the Medina itself, the magnificent 19th-century palace, the Dar Ben Abdallah, is well worth visiting. It is a museum of Tunisian urban life in the late 19th and early 20th centuries and the rooms are not only furnished but have figures in traditional dress which combine to make it the ideal way of learning something about embroideries in context. A similar arrangement on a very much smaller scale can be seen at the Musée du Bardo on the outskirts of Tunis. As we have mentioned, a number of the local museums also have costumes. The C.A.T.P. at the Bey's Palace in Carthage have an excellent teaching collection of Tunisian costumes and embroideries (as well as other arts and crafts) on which the C.T.F.T. is in part based. It is not open to the general public, but the organisation is most generous about allowing access to scholars.

Ibn Khaldun on Tunis

"In the Maghreb, the arts are few and, apart from the weaving of wool, the tanning of leather and sewing, imperfect..."

Ibn Khaldun goes on to explain that this is because these were skills most necessary and most natural to the nomads who had invaded the country. He then discusses the perfection to which the arts had been brought in Cairo and Spain, and continues:

"Tunisians would sometimes live in Cairo for a number of years and when they came back would bring with them from Egypt the habit of luxury and a knowledge of the perfection of the arts of the Orient, which caused them to be highly regarded. And it is for this reason that in the arts Tunis resembles Cairo, as it also resembles the cities of Spain, because most of its people are descendants of those from Eastern Spain who came as refugees during the movements of the 7th century AH/13th century AD.

"It was in this way that the arts have been preserved at Tunis, and although the city is no longer today at the level of civilization which befits it, nevertheless, once a dye has truly stained a cloth it rarely vanishes until the cloth itself is destroyed."

The embroidery

As the fascinating work on Tunisian costume, *C.T.F.T.*, previously mentioned, points out, the embroidered marriage costume of the provincial towns provides an anthology of the clothes of Tunis in the 18th and 19th centuries. The purple Turkish-style caftan still worn at Hammamet is essentially that of 18th- to mid-19th-century Tunis and the golden tunic found in a number of places, especially in the Sahel, was in the late 19th-century fashion. Again, the early 19th-century everyday dress included a very short parti-coloured tunic in emerald/purplish red, a version of which is still to be seen at Le Kef and elsewhere. Since Tunis was famous — or perhaps notorious — for its luxury and its women's passion for clothes, it might be logical to discuss the magnificent originals rather than the provincial copies. Since, however, the Tunis versions are now purely museum pieces, I have chosen to describe these robes, particularly in terms of embroidery, in the sections on the towns where they have survived, albeit tenuously, to the present.

The Tunis embroidery tradition was naturally very mixed. An Andalusian past, real or imagined, a Turkish presence and an active trade brought all kinds of influences over the centuries.

"The women of Tunis are very well dressed and attractively got-up. It is true that they cover their faces, as do the women of Fez. They hide them by putting a very wide band of material across their foreheads and over it another veil called *sefseri*, so that they seem to have giants' heads. They are only interested in their toilettes and their scents — so much so that the scent shops are always the last to close."

Leo Africanus, 16th century

The giants' head style of veiling was still in use early this century.

The *sefseri* remains the standard Tunisian veil. The scent shops still seem to be open more than any of the others.

Turkish and Balkan embroidery

The question of Turkish and Balkan embroidery in North Africa has largely been dealt with under Algeria. I have never seen great curtains of the Algerian type from Tunisia, but pieces of embroidery in the Turkish manner and following the Turkish custom were used to decorate the bridal chamber. Turkish towels are quite often found, not generally of very fine workmanship and therefore probably of local manufacture rather than imported from the capital. This is, however, a matter which has been much discussed (see bibliography).

Mid and late 19th-century Tunis evolved a costume which I personally find most inelegant. So, apparently, did Hesse-Warteg writing in 1882:

> "The costume of the Jewesses is as ugly as the costume of the Jews has been shown to be picturesque and beautiful. Seen from a distance, Jewesses resemble ballet-girls, of whose body the upper part was wrapped in a sack down to the hips. The stranger who meets such a figure for the first time fancies he sees a woman who has forgotten to dress herself, and is rather perplexed.... Over the upper part of the body a baggy chemise falls down to the hips, made of red, yellow or light green silk, and their head is covered by the velvet 'kufia' embroidered in gold and shaped like a sugar-loaf, and is tied by a red or yellow silk ribbon...."

Except that the colours varied according to fashion, this is a very good description of the dress of all well-to-do women in Tunis at that period. The style of the later 19th century, for Muslim women on grand occasions, included trousers baggy at the top and tight in the calf, not unlike jodhpurs. They were called *sirwal bed-duka* and the long triangles of embroidery rising up the outer side of the leg certainly echo the shape of the conical headdress – *duka*. This needlework was some of the finest and most charming done in Tunisia and it is a great pity that it is not imitated or revived today. The motifs are floral, often with a pair of birds, one on each knee, usually monochrome or in soft colours, and the stitches and the general appearance of the work suggest a very strong Balkan (*C.T.F.T.* specifies Albanian) influence.

The *duka* headdress is also interesting. Magnificently embroidered in gold, it is a small version of the very high metal cone worn by the married women of Algeria last century. The *sarma*, as it is called is comparable to the *tantoura* of the Druze women of the Lebanon and to our mediaeval hennin — brought back from the Levant during the Crusades, perhaps? Over the *sarma* was draped a transparent silk veil, again richly embroidered, as a rule with gold.

Gold embroidery and embroidery on leather

These two subjects are not dealt with in depth in this book, although they are among the commonest forms of embroidery all along the North African coast. They have been omitted because they should either be discussed in great detail (see bibliography for various excellent articles) or else a brief review, such as has been given for Fez in Morocco, is true in a general way for the whole area. Again, gold embroidery on velvet was sometimes done by men and that on leather normally was, and hence falls outside the main scope of this work.

Gold embroidery from Tunis — although similar patterns are found from Cairo to Rabat. The lobed outer circle is known as "circle of the moon". The alternating lobes and points inside are the "seal" and the star in the centre "heart of the seal". The palmettes are "two thirds of an apple" and the flowers between them "marjoram", while those on the outside are "jasmine".

There certainly has been a long tradition of gold embroidery in North Africa, but there is every reason to think that in its present form it is largely of Turkish inspiration – and hence the homogeneity of style from Rabat to Tripoli, and even Cairo. The Turks were particularly fond of embroidered trappings and accoutrements (see Fez p.41) so much so that Mehmed Efendi, the ambassador from the Sublime Porte to Louis XV in 1721, numbered them among his official gifts to the king, who was still a child:

> "First, a horse from Mytilene, harnessed with royal trappings. Its saddle and housing were of a white cloth, embroidered with gold thread, worked with a number of colours and of admirable craftsmanship....Secondly, a quiver full of very pretty little arrows and a small bow equally well made. The quiver too was decorated with a very fine piece of embroidery in drawn gold...."

Third – predictably – came lengths of material, furs and scent.

Embroidery on men's clothes

"For the Malikis God is Great, for the Hanafis God is Beautiful."
Tunisian proverb contrasting two of the four
schools of religious law

*   *   *

Very little has been said in this book about traditional men's clothes, principally because the embroidered as opposed to woven pieces (*burnous, jebba*, etc) have almost entirely vanished, as is generally the case, men being less conservative than women in such matters. The exception is the little boy's circumcision costume, which has been mentioned briefly in the sections on Fez and Sousse.

The two remaining types of embroidery intended for men are certain articles of gold embroidery (again see Fez p.42; in Tunisia these things have become much less current) and the self-coloured couched and braided patterns highlighted by needlework which make up a kind of raised embroidery known as *tahlil*, used around the necks of tunics – *juha*, caftans and *fraja* – a caftan-shaped over-garment. These three worn one above the other and often sold in matching sets, are of Turkish, or perhaps ultimately Persian, origin and today are worn almost exclusively by scholars and men of religion, in particular those following the Hanafi school of law. Unlike the indigenous Tunisian clothes, these, derived in both shape and decoration from Turkish military uniforms, are elaborately cut and shaped and carefully finished.

The decoration is largely around the neck and really involves a kind of passementerie rather than embroidery, and is comparable to our "frogging". A favourite motif on the breast of the *juha* is the *Shamsa*, halfway between the sun and a flower, and said, appropriately, to symbolize the light of religion.

Another very common motif, particularly on the breast of the caftan is a kind of Kashmiri "cone", which in Tunisia forms a pseudo-pocket, but on Indian or Persian robes is often a real one in which one could keep some small valuable. A similar motif is frequently to be found on the *farmla*, or sleeveless jacket, worn by boys on the occasion of their circumcision, while the *chechia* or fez more usually has the crescent, a floral motif or something clearly deriving from an Ottoman military device.

The sleeves, side-seams and buttons of these robes also provide scope for North Africa's admirable braids, ribbons, tassels, needlework buttons and so on. The insides of these robes too are beautifully finished, with silk linings appliquéd on to the inner lining, often in what is called a "swallow wing" pattern. In Morocco what looks like a seven branched candlestick is also found and a five-pronged "hand", or, much more rarely a crescent and star. These Moroccan caftans are, incidentally, quite different from the very subdued plain wool or neutral silk still worn in Tunisia and are much closer to their Turkish originals. They were extraordinarily gorgeous, in the most brilliant and sumptuous silks that could be woven locally or imported from Italy, France or the Levant, and all the braiding was, of course, in gold.

Appliqué was also used on the very handsome woollen burnouses — *kebba* — worn by notables on important occasions in Tunisia. The outside was some sober colour, often black, but the entire lining was a patchwork appliqué designed to show when the end was tossed over the shoulder in the approved manner. A particularly splendid one in the Dar Ben Abdallah in Tunis is black embroidery of the Mahdia type around the neck opening. The hood has a black silk tassel nearly a foot long. Inside there is an asymmetric patchwork lining in chiefly crimson damask, yellow brocade and purple velvet with piping along all the joins and a complicated braided edging.

Sequin embroidery

"I have a caftan all sewn with pearls
And it cannot be compared with any other
                                              girl's"
A couplet put into the mouth of Aziza Othmana,
which has become a proverb. She was the
much-loved daughter of the Bey Othman and her
good works – including founding Tunis' hospital –
were famous. Her tomb can be seen in the Medina.

Towards the end of the 19th century, inspired by the fashion of
the Bey's court, there came into existence the form of wedding
dress still favoured today – indeed, together with the white European dress, it is tending to spread all over the country to the
detriment of the various regional styles.

This particular dress – again, to my eyes, far less attractive than
most of the regional ones – consists of enormous pantaloons,
which may measure up to 4.5 m round the waist, and a bolero top,
low-cut with large puff sleeves. Since the bride is supposed to have
a fine bosom, it is wired out and stiffened to most impressive
proportions. One that I measured appeared to be 46DD. The gap
between the bottom of the bolero and the top of the trousers is often
filled, in the interests of modesty, with pink or white nylon. It has
become customary to surmount the whole with a Western-style
wedding veil, often of traditional hand-embroidered tulle. Earlier a
kind of pill-box cap would have been worn. Matching furnishings
also used to be prepared – cushions for the bride's throne or covers
for the dower chests, for example, but this custom has almost
entirely lapsed.

The wedding dress is covered with sequin embroidery of a very
distinctive type, which seems to be peculiar to Tunisia, in particular
to Tunis and the coast. As regards the trousers and skirts, it is rare to
find complete pieces. A dealer in the Medina of Tunis told me the
following in 1972 – I have no idea whether it is generally true:

> "In my mother's day [1920s or 1930s], when a girl
> got married, her mother took an ingot of silver to one
> of the Jews who made sequins and *alkantir* [spiral
> tubular beads – the word comes from the Spanish
> *canutillo* – little reed]. He then would give an equal
> weight of sequins, keeping a percentage for his

trouble. If she wanted them gold-washed, she would also take a piece of gold. Then she would buy good heavy satin, or pure silk, not like today, and would take all these things to the embroideress. The design would be chosen after much discussion with her friends. Everything would be done well in advance, to give time to pay and also because in the past there was no hurry.

After the girl's marriage, she would put her wedding clothes away in her dower chest. She would feel very romantic. Even if times were hard, she would not want to part with them. Later, after her first child, she might lend them to a neighbour or a younger sister. When she grew old, she would no longer care. She would think – the silver is valuable, and when she wanted to buy a piece of land or modern ornaments for her own daughter's mar- riage, she would take her wedding clothes back to the Jewish sequin-maker and he would give her the value of the silver, keeping a percentage for his trouble. But first she would cut off a strip to show her daughters the pattern and for the memory. That is why I have only pieces in my shop."

I asked whether the cloth was burned to retrieve the silver, as is done with saris in India, but he did not know. He added, however:

"The work they do today is worthless. The sequins are tin or plastic and as light as air; just like the women, who are like rattling bones. When I married my wife, her dress was so heavy she could not walk alone and, although I was a strong man, I could not have lifted her on to a mule's back."

One interesting point about these wedding clothes – as we have explained elsewhere, they are far from being the exclusive preroga- tive of the rich. For people who cannot afford to commission a set, there are two options. They can hire them from the go-between (see the *Arabian Nights* for details of this character) or from one of the families who specialise in renting out wedding and feast-day equipment (and whose charges had become so exorbitant in some parts of North Africa that they recently had to be controlled by government decree) or from the *ma'allema* herself. Alternatively, they could rely on the generosity of relatives and even neighbours. The remarks made by Charles Ougouag-Nezzal in his excellent article on "Wedding Clothes and Ornaments of Tlemcen" holds true for all North Africa:

".... the poor bride on her wedding day can show the same lavish wealth, although everyone knows that it is not really hers. Indeed, not only her own clan shows solidarity on this occasion. Simple neighbours as well as relatives, will lend precious jewels or a valuable caftan to the bride who is without. The loan is made for the sake of *adjer*, the divine reward for an action pleasing to God, and the Koranic injunction — 'Woe...to those who refuse aid, help' (*Surah* 107 vv. 4-7) — is used to reinforce what is probably a much older commandment. It is on account of these values, still alive today, that a little girl may be found running from one house to another through the ancient streets of Tlemcen, carrying a fortune in clothes and jewels made into the humblest-looking bundle, as a loan to some poor orphan."

Woman's wedding jacket — farmla — from Tunis. Early 20th century

To return to Tunisian wedding clothes. The skirts and trousers are usually worked on heavy satin backed with strong cotton, generally of the same colour. In the past, the favourite colours were purple, plum, violet, lavender, bluish-grey, grey, olive, brown, russet and black. More recently, pale pink, pale blue and white seem to have become fashionable. The mules and jacket were made to match, although they are almost never found. Much the most common jackets are worked on black, dark red or midnight blue velvet. I do not know whether these simply happen to have survived better, or whether there was at some time a fashion for wearing velvet jackets with satin trousers. These velvet jackets are of the sleeveless bolero type. In any case, it is rare to see anything like a complete set of these wedding clothes.

Sequin embroidery is done on a low rectangular frame, *gourgaf* – the word is Turkish. It is said that traditionally the embroideresses could work out their designs freehand, but many of them are so complicated that it seems unlikely this was always true. I, personally, have never seen an example in which the pattern was traced or drawn on to the material, but often there is a layer of strong paper between the satin and the backing and this may have been cut to provide the design as well as support for the cloth. Another technique which I have seen used is pricking out the design (in this case the embroideress was copying an old piece) a little at a time with a needle, which marks the material just enough to provide a guideline.

The sewing thread, often linen, is very strong, as it needs to be in order to support the weight of the sequins, which never seem to come adrift, and it is normally the same colour as the satin. In any case, it can only be seen from the back, which, although obviously not meant to be looked at, gives the effect of quilting.

The embroideress brings her needle up through the hole in the sequin (which is roughly 3 mm in diameter), picks up a piece of *alkantir* (usually 2-3 mm long) and then takes the needle back through the hole in the sequin to the reverse of the work. Alternatively, in order to cover flat areas and to give extra sheen, the sequins are sewn overlapping, so that the holes cannot be seen, without intervening *alkantir*.

The beauty of this work lies in the surprising number of textures obtainable with two basic elements and two techniques; very occasionally, a play of gold and silver is added. In a bunch of grapes, for example, shade will be indicated by grapes worked entirely in lines of *alkantir*, which is not really luminous, while on the "light" side of the bunch sequins are arranged in concentric circles catching the light. Lines of *alkantir* vein the leaves and make up the tendrils, while a broad shining river below is made by the overlapping technique.

The designs, too, are interesting, and it would be nice to know a great deal more about them. Unlike other traditional forms of embroidery, there is a considerable variety and the inspiration seems very mixed. Geometrical designs – stars, stylized daisies, twisting ribbons – are quite common; but so are motifs perhaps

Sequin grape-vine pattern from a Turkish wedding dress, early 20th century

copied from the Classical and palaeo-Christian marbles which are scattered all over the country, such as vines and pomegranates. Paired birds, doves or peacocks, beside a vase or chalice – a very favourite Tunisian marriage theme which reappears on chests and paintings on glass – are very common on the jackets. Surprisingly, fish (the ancient fertility symbol of the area) and hands (the hand of Fatima which averts misfortune) are not particularly common, although small embroidered three-dimensional fish can sometimes be bought and their modern equivalent, decorated with ribbons, tinsel and gold paper, can be found everywhere.

I once saw a length of sequin embroidery with a pattern of storks and chrysanthemums. Storks are very popular in North Africa, and indeed in Morocco people try to "steal" each other's storks and the good luck they bring. In this case, however, the stylization suggested very strongly that a Japanese pattern had been copied – perhaps from a cotton *yukata*, or something of the kind.

Other common and more predictable motifs are stylized carnations and tulips, clearly of Turkish inspiration, and, particularly beautiful, are the "teardrops" from the prized Kashmiri shawls. The range has nothing much to do with other embroidery, even other gold embroidery of North Africa, and would well repay study, before all the pieces have gone to make evening purses and have been irretrievably scattered.

The fate of sequin embroidery today is rather sad, although it is much used for expensive wedding and evening dresses. Indeed, a Western-style white wedding dress, which, it should be remembered is a relative innovation for us too, is often worn in Tunis instead of traditional clothes and elsewhere will probably figure as one of the changes which the bride displays.

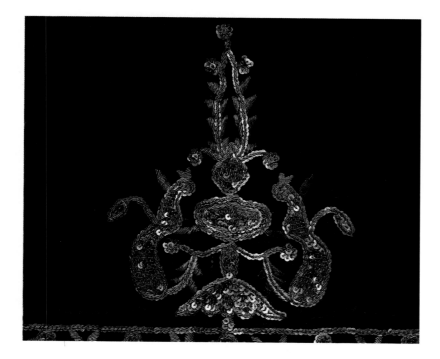

Details of the peacocks and vase motif from the back of a velvet jacket. Tunis, early 20th century. The dove and vase version of this is said to have originated in the Greek world about the 3rd century B.C.

Two Ma'allema

A mistress-embroideress I spoke to in her shop in Sousse in the late 1970s was doing work technically as fine as any of the older pieces, but, as she herself said, working with rather large plastic sequins on nylon was *not* the same. The pinks and blues, mixed with little beads then very fashionable, were garish rather than luxurious and the shape of Western dresses tended to demand heavy bands on the bodice, sometimes with the pattern curling round the breasts in an unfortunate way, rather than the rich over-all designs of the traditional marriage clothes. The result was tawdry and, of course, in the West sequins, unless used very carefully, tend to suggest night-clubs more than anything else.

Asked whether she could and would work with the old heavy silver sequins, she said, willingly, if I could find her some. I asked why they were no longer available and she repeated what I had heard before: they were made by Jews and the Jews had all gone away. I imagine the rocketing price of silver also had something to do with it, although a very debased kind was commonly used. I enquired whether it would be possible to reuse old sequins and was told that it would not be satisfactory. Firstly, the silver tarnishes a little with time and cannot be cleaned and secondly both the sequins and the *alkantir* bend slightly in working and cannot be straightened.

A Tunis *ma'allema* in the autumn of 1983 told me that while prices vary very much, the cost of a particular set of wedding clothes displayed in her window would be the equivalent of £1,400 and that to hire them for the wedding would be between £140 and £350 depending (I gathered) on how long the celebrations lasted. The price included her putting in an appearance to arrange the bride's clothes, but not to henna her hands or dress her hair. She told me that the beauticians who performed these services often also rented clothes, but they "would not be of the quality of mine". Hers were, indeed, in their way, very splendid. She told me that she had at that time eight apprentices in various stages of training and that a set consisting of trousers, bolero and headdress or veil, with slippers and bags for the bride to put her hands in while the henna is setting, would take six to nine months to make. The only point on which she was reticent was her patterns and I did not manage to find out whether she drew them herself or whether they were copied from books. Clearly she considered her designs as being professional secrets — although she was perfectly happy, indeed very pleased, to have the finished pieces photographed.

Sequin embroidery, history and types

*   *   *

"Russet satyn spangled with spangles of fine
gold"
Hollinshed's Chronicle. *Henry VIII*. 1548

*   *   *

Sequin embroidery is in fact mentioned in England in the 13th century, but the word "sequin", which is Arabic, did not come into use until a hundred years ago and the term by which they were known as "spangle".

The origin of this kind of embroidery is not very clearly under-stood, but there are some fine early examples in Spain, for example the magnificent chasuble of Her Most Catholic Majesty, Queen Isabella, offered by her husband, Ferdinand of Aragon, to the Cathedral of Granada in 1492. Certainly it seems possible that sequin embroidery reached North Africa with the immigrants from Spain in the 16th and 17th centuries, although, as I have stressed, it also has a great deal in common with analogous work from Turkey and the Eastern Mediterranean. Sequin embroidery is, incidentally, still used in Spain today for the clothes worn by the bullfighters and for the robes and trappings of the Madonnas carried by the Confraternities in the Easter Week processions.

Sequins are used in the embroidery of a number of North African towns – Algiers, Tlemcen, Fez – to enrich work basically done in gold or silver thread. Often the sequins, spaced in rows or other patterns, are used as a filling inside certain of the larger motifs as a relief from plain couching. This kind of use is also made of them in some Turkish embroidery and dark velvets, or else heavy satin, are the most common backgrounds. Work of this type is found in Tunisia, especially on the girls' and women's headdresses and occasionally on little boys' circumcision clothes.

It is, however, the more distinctive type of embroidery done almost entirely in sequins and a speciality of Tunisia, and in particular of Tunis and the coastal towns, that we have, for the most part, been considering here.

By the way, the kinds of embroidery on muslin, or fine cotton or linen involving thin flat strips of tinsel are never, as far as I know, North African, although they are sometimes sold as such. The ones in which the strips are mixed with coloured silks to make stylized floral patterns are for the most part 19th-century Turkish towels, although some in fact come from Syria, and there is always the possibility that they were local imitations. The scarves, usually black, white or pale blue, with a fantastic weight of silver for the fineness of the cloth, and geometric, architectural or very, very formal flower patterns, are Egyptian and mostly date from the 1920s and 1930s when they seem to have been popular souvenirs. The thin flat metal thread is used quite extensively in Tunisia, but in a rather different way. It either appears on the woollen gauze dresses worn at Hammamet and elsewhere, or else on heavy silk or satin, particularly for headdresses, for example the reversible scarves of Ksar Hellal. For these last a long-eyed needle is used, but in general *tal* is worked without a needle, the thread being simply pushed back and forth through the rather loosely woven cloth. This is not as easy as it sounds, because the metal is soft and bends and

Plastron of mwasma *tunic from Raf-Raf*

twists easily. It is almost impossible to straighten it neatly and if it is carelessly handled the gilding wears off the gold varieties.

I have no idea how to date sequin embroidery. The pieces offered for sale seem to me to run from the end of the 19th century to the middle of the 20th. I have seen few that I thought might be earlier than the second half of the 19th century. Of course, when the costume is intact it is easier to tell. It is true that the most elaborately worked-out designs using tiny sequins tend to be the most worn and tarnished, but whether this really means that they are older, or, being more beautiful, have been borrowed more often, I do not know. It would be fascinating to find out.

*   *   *

"God is beautiful and He loves beauty."

Tunisian Proverb

*   *   *

Turkish Embroideries

(AND EMBROIDERIES IN THE TURKISH MANNER)

TURKISH EMBROIDERIES IN NORTH AFRICA

One of the main influences on the embroideries of North Africa was, very naturally, Turkey — there was a Turkish presence for some three centuries and Istanbul, although never as glamorous in local eyes as Andalusia, did set fashions in much the way that Paris was to do later.

The influence of Turkey is seen very clearly in all the goldwork, and also in the shapes of certain of the costumes, the wedding caftans of Hammamet and Sousse, for example. There is indeed, in Tunis a Souk et-Trouk, or "Souk of the Turks", where originally Turkish embroiderers and tailors, or embroiderers and tailors working in the Turkish manner, had their shops.

There is also Turkish or Balkan influence in some of the silk embroideries, very notably those of Algiers and Chéchaouen, the white and pale blue work of Nabeul, and on some of the 19th-century costumes from Tunis.

It is worth comparing these floral sprays worked into squares from a 19th century Turkish towel with some of the motifs from Fez, Meknes, Sale and elsewhere

Thirdly, there are quite large quantities of purely Turkish embroidery to be found in North Africa, both in museums and offered for sale. Most often they are the small pieces which in England are generally known as "Turkish towels", although they may in fact be sashes, draw-strings and side panels of trousers, cushion covers, carrying cloths, chest covers, headscarves and so on. I have also seen fragments of what were clearly larger pieces, probably hangings, or possibly bed covers, but, by chance, have never found a whole one, although there must have been a good number made for the palaces of the beys and the households of the wealthy.

There is a good deal of argument as to whether these Turkish embroideries were actually made in North Africa or whether they were imported. I think the problem is almost impossible to solve, since, as we have seen, embroidery is inclined to be a very tradition-al skill and there is no reason to think that a Turkish woman who changed countries would embroider, at least initially, any different-ly in Tunis or Algiers than she had in Istanbul and Bursa. Clearly, in time she or her descendants would be influenced by local taste and the sense of the fashions and style of the capital would become dulled with the years. The best one can do is to say that the rather rough pieces are in all likelihood produced locally, while the — extremely rare — fine examples were luxury goods imported from Turkey. But even this conjecture is only a matter of probability.

Turkish towels are easily recognisable among the other North African embroideries. Much the most common type is worked on white or natural cotton or linen, generally rectangular, with a strip of needlework at each of the narrow ends. The designs are usually stylized but recognisable flowers or fruit, one motif often being repeated with variants, and the colours tend to be more delicate than in the native work. There are other kinds. For example that with dark pomegranate or madder red and indigo blue predominating, very similar to the Algiers curtains, and it is to this variety that the larger fragments generally belong. The pieces found in North Africa are almost always 19th- and very occasionally late 18th-century. I am not aware of having seen anything older.

Hyacinth and pomegran-ate design from a North African Turkish "towel".

Since Turkish towels, besides being of importance to North African embroidery both in themselves and as influences, are also very attractive and much prized in the West today, it seems worth saying a little bit about them.

Turkish Towels

Anyone examining an ordinary old-fashioned towel will notice a smooth band, a few inches from either end. It now serves no function — it is not even decorative — but is left over from the time when that position was occupied by some of the most beautiful and elegant embroidery ever made.

The Turkish towel has a long history and is only by chance known to us as "Turkish", since the objects were in common use all over the Islamic World from Saudi Arabia to North Africa, and fine examples have been highly prized in the West for centuries. The true Turkish towel, as it is known today, was made of a cotton material woven in loops to increase its absorbency, and the technique seems to have been invented about 1800, possibly in Syria. This kind of towel consisted of a strip about 80cm × 1.5m with at either end a band of plain weave about 25cm from the bottom to take the embroidery, and a fringe.

Although the actual technique of weaving in loops is comparatively new, towels naturally existed long before – public, and for that matter private, baths having always been very much a feature of Islamic city life. Indeed, some of the simplest towels are marked along the band with the name of the *hammam* and sometimes a request that the towel should not be removed! Before the invention of looped towelling, other ingenious methods of increasing the absorbency of the material were devised: weaving in thick linen threads at intervals to roughen the surface, or making raised or tufted patches – checks, spots, chevrons, and so on for the same purpose.

Earlier still, in the late 17th and 18th centuries, there was a tendency to use very large pieces of muslin – to dry oneself. A traveller described them as "a degree finer than steam vapour", which sounds very like the classical stuffs "woven of the wind", or the transparent veils of Cos worn by Cleopatra; in less romantic terms, the towels might have as many as 80 threads to the inch. In spite of its fineness, the material was extraordinarily strong, for at this period the decorated band would be a solid mass of flowers and arabesques in delicately shaded silks, enriched with filaments of pure silver, plain or gold-washed, wrapped round a core of thread, with the result that the ends might weigh fifty or sixty times the basic material of the towel – and yet the handwoven cotton never tears, even after centuries.

It was almost certainly towels of this type that Alexander Russell mentions in his, inevitably second-hand, description of the women's baths at Aleppo around 1700:

End of a fine Turkish towel, late 18th century. The work is very similar to that on the kettafiya *– 'shoulder piece' from Tétouan, Algiers.*

"They then wrap their hair in a fine piece of muslin with a worked border, and, embroidered in the middle with gold flowers, which is called massar shiar — 'hair squeezer'. The head is attired in the manner of a Turban with a kind of fine towel, made at Constantinople…"

Russell adds that when the bath was completed, the servants would tie up the damp linen in another embroidered cloth and that finely embroidered towels, hair covers, and so on were considered an essential part of an elegant woman's equipment.

The word "towel" should not, perhaps, be taken too literally. In the English of Chaucer's day the word could be used to apply to a napkin, wrapping, or even head covering, and the same is probably true of many of the pieces which now pass as towels, although they would naturally have had specific names in Arabic or Turkish at the period they were in use.

Beautifully embroidered wrappings and coverings are a very old tradition in the Islamic world — none, of course more splendid than the *kiswa* or veil of the Ka'aba at Mecca. Similarly, it was the custom to wrap up Korans and other precious books, and later decrees, or *fatwahs*, of the ruler were often presented in layers of decorated cloth; some of those belonging to the Turkish Sultans being splendidly marked with their *tughra* or signature. Presents were similarly given — the girls of Aleppo had the charming custom of making bouquets using a "language of flowers" and sending them wrapped in an embroidered handkerchief. Again, this century, when the cupboards of the Topkapi Serai were opened, the robes of the Sultans were found put away in as many as forty layers of embroidered cloth — and in perfect condition.

Part of this use of embroidered cloths goes back to Byzantine times, where they had a ceremonial, as well as practical, function: on festival days, the Emperor would mark the start of the races at the Hippodrome by throwing down an official starting napkin, richly decorated, from the imperial box. There is no exact parallel for this in the Muslim world, but the diplomat de Busbecq mentions towels being offered as prizes in a shooting contest near Pera in 1562:

"The competition is carried out in a most orderly manner and in complete silence, in spite of the huge crowd of spectators. The bows which they use on this occasion are very stiff, and can only be bent by archers who are very well trained. They also have special arrows. The reward of victory is an embroidered towel..."

On less reliable authority, it is said that an embroidered towel was given to the favourite of the Sultan to indicate that she had been chosen by him. This may or not be true, but certainly in Greece as well as Turkey, a distinctively embroidered towel was prepared by a bride as part of her trousseau for use on her wedding night, after which it was carefully preserved, unlaundered, in case of dispute. The witnesses, who would have examined it, were very naturally thought more likely to be able to recognize a piece of embroidery than a plain length of cloth and these towels were therefore of legal importance, the decoration being considered as individual as a signature.

Foreigners visiting the Middle East were struck by the magnificence of the embroidery put to very humble uses and this level of luxury was commented on again and again. Perhaps it is not surprising in the context of a world in which the Grand Vizir could say after the terrible defeat at Lepanto:

"Lord Admiral, the wealth and power of the Empire is such that if it is necessary we can make anchors of silver, cables of silk and sails of satin..."

And his boast was true!

Lady Mary Wortley Montague, a great traveller in the Middle East, wrote almost 150 years later of dinner in the house of Sultana Hafiten:

"...the magnificence of her table answered well to that of her dress. The knives were gold, the hafts set with diamonds. But the piece of luxury that grieved my eyes was the table-cloth and napkins, which are all tiffany, embroidered with silks and gold, in the finest manner, in natural flowers. It was with great regret that I made use of these costly napkins, as finely wrought as the finest handkerchiefs that ever came out of our country. You may be sure that they were entirely spoiled before the dinner was over. The sherbet (which is the liquor they drink at meals) was served in china bowls; but the covers and salvers massy gold. After dinner, water was brought in a gold basin, and towels of the same kind as the napkins, which I very unwillingly wiped my hands upon; and coffee was served in china, with gold soucoupes."

Another writer nearer our own day was of the same opinion and adds that of all the luxuries she admired in the East, the thing she most coveted were the towels and table linen.

Relatively naturalistic flowers, including rose and cyclamen, from 19th century Turkish towel. Note the difference in colour sense between real Turkish work and that of North Africa

There has been a great deal of discussion as to where and by whom these embroideries were produced. Constantinople is generally agreed to have been the main centre, but the fashion spread all over the Islamic world and also to Greece, Yugoslavia, the Balkans and other areas within the Turkish sphere of influence. One thing is certain: they were not factory-produced like Egyptian *tiraz* or Damascus silks and hence there are very few records. Probably the bulk were made at home, for, as a general rule, whenever women were secluded and had a degree of affluence very fine embroideries were produced. This is hardly surprising: the women had unlimited leisure and the embroidery provided them with a means of self-expression, hence each piece is highly individual, not copied from a pattern book, and two identical pieces are never found, except as a set, until well on in the 19th century. There is also the economic aspect. It is recorded at Cairo and Constantinople that women who were not professional seamstresses would do fine embroidery for pocket-money, entrusting it to a *dallala* – or middle-woman – to sell in the souks.

An early reference, apparently to this kind of work, is found in Marco Polo, writing of Kerman then under Tartar rule:

> "The gentlewomen and their daughters are adepts with the needle, embroidering silk of all colours with beasts and birds and many other figures. They embroider the curtains of nobles and great men so well and so richly that they are a delight to the eye. And they are no less skilful at working counterpanes, cushions and pillows."

A 16th-century traveller in Turkey describes these "towels" worn as headcloths and thrown around the shoulders very much in the manner of the draperies of Classical Greece, and, specifically in Constantinople, both this and the face veil were known as *yashmak*. It is not unlikely that the custom was carried on from Byzantium, for paintings and mosaics show noble ladies wearing stoles in a very similar way. All those who saw them were very much impressed with the fineness and colourfulness of the work, and we know from the records of various import-export companies that supply never met demand. Oriental embroideries, like carpets, were apt to be the show-pieces of any household. Mary of Burgundy, the wife of the German Emperor Maximilian I, had four Turkish bolster covers proudly mentioned in an inventory of her effects and, a century later, the Arch-Duchess Marie Christine was to write to her mother "it is only a simple ribbon and plain, but am sending it because I know well enough that Your Highness likes Turkish things."

Unfortunately, little survives from this date. Early towels are, for the most part, not very large, about 45cm × 1.2m, of pure unpatterned linen, embroidered in silk or tightly twisted wool. The colours are usually simple: natural, white, pure brilliant reds and blues produced from the madder and indigofera indigenous to the Levant, and black. This last was least satisfactory, for the dye was essentially made from iron and vinegar, which was apt to turn rust-coloured with time and make the thread very brittle. Occasionally, however, especially in Kurdish territory, the black will be found to have remained beautifully shiny and glossy. This is because the embroideress has used her hair instead of silk — a motif which appears in our Arthurian romances, where one of the Queen's maidens uses her golden hair when sewing shirts for the Knights of the Round Table and so begins a love story which is eventually to prove tragic.

Towels from the early period usually have simple conventionalised flower patterns and often a single design unit is repeated to fill the space. Occasionally the decoration is calligraphic — sometimes phrases from the Koran, which suggests they were used for performing the ablutions, perhaps in the mosque, and sometimes with good-luck phrases — "blessings", "peace be upon you", and so on. At this date, the words usually form a plain band, but later more complicated inscriptions were often arranged in highly decorative patterns, for example one word set in each square of a chequerboard.

Evliya Chelebi, a nobleman writing about AH 1048/AD 1638 says that in Constantinople there were 65 men embroiderers selling their output in 20 shops, and another 25 specialising in handkerchiefs, towels, sheets, etc. Since this was a very small number of craftsmen for such a vast city as Constantinople, it must be assumed that the bulk of the production was domestic and that the shops basically catered to people from out of town and to tourists. Interestingly, Evliya adds, after his description of the relevant guild: "My mother was famous in this handicraft."

Russell, again writing of Aleppo, says of the girls:

> "When about seven years old, they are sent to school to learn to sew and embroider: but their work in embroidery is greatly inferior to that of the Constantinople ladies. The handkerchiefs of the men are embroidered with silk and various colours, as well as with gold and silver; and are common presents made by the women, in the same manner as worked watch cases, purses and tobacco bags."

From the end of the 17th century, the designs had become more graceful, with curves and tendrils, and the number of colours increased. Over the next hundred years, the patterns became more and more complex and flamboyant, and the space tends to be completely filled. There is an effort at perspective and a huge range of very carefully shaded colours, especially pastels, is used, beautifully off-set by the lavish use of thread made of precious metals. By far the most common designs are floral: tulips, roses, carnations, hyacinths, lilies and forget-me-nots being among the most popular flowers, and apples, pomegranates, peaches and grapes the favourite fruit, with the occasional snail or insect. Realism, however, was not important, and the flowers are often so stylized as to be barely recognisable. These flowers developed into gardens and one particularly charming pattern is known as "the kiosk and cypress". It is just that, but often there is a formalized view of the Bosphorus, complete with boats, flowering almonds and weeping willows — a kind of Turkish willow pattern. Occasionally there are even one or two little figures, but this is rare at Constantinople, where orthodoxy was observed, and are generally from the remoter provinces, or even from the Greek Islands which were long under Turkish rule and produced work which is technically very similar to that from the mainland.

Detail of a Turkish sash

It is, in fact, hard to know just where any piece came from. There are indications: Bursa, for example, specialised in open work using much flat tinsel, Malatya had a distinctive type of chain stitch, and it has been suggested that the pieces with bold red and blue flowers are from the Iznik region, because of their similarity to the tiles and other ceramics made there. Patterns and techniques were, however, both copied and exported all over the Islamic world and it would be hard to swear where a piece bought today in Jiddah or Tunis was actually made.

Later 19th-century towels tend to be less fine, the patterns are confused and, at least from the middle of the century, imported Western dyes resulted in some very ugly and harsh colour combinations. Again instead of fine real silver and gilt thread, large areas of flashy tinsel are used, generally made of coated copper. There were also the twin problems of declining wealth and declining leisure, which gave less scope for this very time-consuming work. Recently, however, the establishment of Girls' Technical Schools in many parts of the Middle East, coupled with a great revival of Islamic arts and crafts, has led to a new interest in this very decorative skill and, I hope this will in turn lead to a new cycle of production, as is happening in the United States and Europe with a number of traditional arts which seemed on the verge of extinction.

Turkish sash showing embroidered border

Stitches and Applications

Stitches
North African Embroidery
uses a relatively restricted
range of stitches, most of
them flat or running rather
than looped, chain or
knotted. Embroideresses
often seem to have been
more interested in getting
a particular effect – say a
neat outline – than using a
particular stitch. Couching,
laid work and appliqué
techniques were also
used.

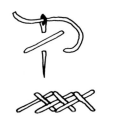

Long-Armed Cross Stitch

El Djem

One major function of a book on embroidery is that it should help those who themselves embroider since it is *they*, not those of us who write, or buy and sell, who are the vital element in providing the source of our interest. The importance of books providing patterns, suggestions and stimulation is particularly great today. As we have seen, in the past embroiderers followed traditional patterns or created their own variants, but today, in most parts of the world, the traditions have died or been seriously interrupted, inevitably with considerable loss. However, there is now a new freedom: to create, experiment and in time to build new aesthetically coherent styles. It is even possible, although it is not a point of view generally taken, that there may be a considerable quantity of fine embroidery yet to come. One of the most important factors for good embroidery, after all, is time – hence the best work has often been done for private satisfaction rather than for money – and although we have entered a period in which high labour costs have made high-quality embroidery a commercial rarity, it is correspondingly a time of ever-increasing leisure. It is in the hope of encouraging those who like to try things for themselves that I have added a brief section suggesting possible uses and adaptations of the North African embroidery styles discussed in the main body of the book. These are, of course, only pointers. Everyone will have their own ideas.

Naturally, different styles are suitable for different levels of competence. Those who have never held a needle before, except to sew on a button, should take courage from the charm and individuality of embroideries from El Djem and Gabès. Although the women who made them had very little technical skill, they succeeded in expressing certain aspects of their environment with a few stitches and some bright colours. These embroideries, virtually the only informal ones in all North Africa, are the least competent as needlework, but the most touching and personal as a human record. They are naive art. In terms of technique, anyone could produce such a piece. The problems lie in selecting motifs, stylizing them into a few telling lines, spacing them in a pleasing way and choosing colours. The Tunisian woman would have a tradition of crafts to help her – weaving, pottery, even tattoos. Perhaps most important, she would have a code of symbols with an instant emotional impact; something we have largely lost. We, therefore, in this age have to make our own decisions, without the help of an inherited cultural instinct. This is difficult, but also exciting. The Englishwoman who decides to pick up a strip of material and record her daughter's wedding or the favourite objects in her house and garden faces choices and problems of taste that her Tunisian counterpart will never know, but in solving them the satisfaction is all the greater.

Technically a little more demanding, but aesthetically simpler, are the embroideries from Fez, and, to some extent, those from Salé. Those of Fez, as has been said before, have been adopted by the Moroccan Artisanats because they are easy to teach, require no choice – and hence no taste – on the part of the embroideress, a very limited range of stitches, are effective and can be used on all sorts of easily saleable household items. Fez patterns come out very nicely when worked in cross-stitch and someone who prefers a fairly unambitious project might take an ordinary plain white cotton or linen face towel (it does not even have to be new) and try working a band of one of the Fez patterns, or a small motif in each corner. It takes an afternoon and transforms a rather ordinary object into something unusual and individual. After all, if I have said that one sees too much Fez embroidery in Morocco, the same is certainly *not* true in Europe! The most traditional colours for Fez embroidery are carmine or indigo. These may seem rather dark for face towels or tea cloths, but people with daring may like to take things a stage further and do their Fez work in black. Black on white, as I have mentioned before, was an English speciality, said to have been introduced to the court of Henry VIII by Catherine of Aragon, and today still looks very elegant and striking. Motifs from the front of a Mahdia tunic could also be borrowed for the same purpose.

Incidentally, unless you are trying to make a copy of a North African embroidery, or mend a piece in your possession (very praiseworthy), there is, obviously, no reason why you should not use the patterns as a starting point for your own ideas. A Fez border worked very large in very heavy thread along the middle and up the edge of white curtains could look splendid and be an inexpensive and quick way of making some cheap material look priceless. Again, a motif from a mattress cover would translate well into woollen tapestry, gros point for a cushion, petit point for a glasses case. Two warnings though which apply generally: it is as well to be discreet when mixing or adding colours and combining designs from different areas is, for some reason, difficult and usually looks a mess.

A type of embroidery easily adapted to the popular wool on canvas work is that from Chéchaouen. The mosaic panels reproduce beautifully as cushions and it would certainly be possible to

Double Back Stitch
This and several other plaited stitches – Herringbone, Cretan etc., are used for details and outlining in Morocco and sometimes on the fronts of Mahdia tunics.

Brick Stitch

Brick Stitch (variant)
Much used at Tétouan zellij

Another variant much used in Turkish embroidery, where it is known as loukoum *as in the sweet* Rahat Loukoum – Turkish Delight.

Darning Stitch used as filling in the Turkish manner (after Mrs Christie p. 116)

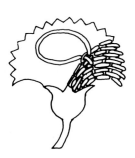

Darning Stitch
Many variants of this basic stitch are used in North African and, particularly, Turkish embroidery, where many kinds of pattern darning are common.

use the patterns to make very pleasant square bags. Again, it would be interesting to try the design for rugs, which might be square using just the mosaic panel, or else to adapt the whole a-b-c-b-a strip as a runner. This could be done in cross-stitch on canvas, a technique not very often used but one which produces pleasing results, or else by using the more usual knotting.

There is one rather curious point about Chéchaouen embroidery: it has already been compared to some of the weaving from Daghestan, but Ulrich Schürmann in his work *Oriental Carpets* (Octopus, London 1979) shows on p.191 a photograph of what appears to be a piece from Chéchaouen and comments:

> "It is not easy to guess the original purpose of this narrow piece of embroidery worked in silk on linen. Most probably the medallion lay on a table or a plinth, or perhaps a prayer desk, whilst the two ends, each embroidered with a prayer arch design, hung down on either side. The yellow panel stands out from the red filigree work and is unlike most other Caucasian work both for its delicacy of line and the unusual nature of its motifs. Another unusual feature is that the two rectangles embroidered on the same background are differently drawn."

This certainly offers room for speculation on the relationship between Chéchaouen and the Caucasus: possibly the ubiquitous Circassian slaves? Therefore using a Chéchaouen pattern to make a carpet might not be particularly anomalous after all.

Chéchaouen Square

Somewhat more complicated still is the embroidery from Raf-Raf. It is extremely cheerful and the basic wool embroidery is not difficult. Isolated motifs could very well be reproduced in the centre of a cushion, on a black wool or felt jacket, or at the ends of a long scarf. Again, a band might be copied to make a belt, an edging to a black skirt or a decoration for the yoke of a child's dress — in red and white striped cotton for the authentically minded! The addition of gold is undoubtedly very attractive, but it is most important that the gold sequins or thread should be of good quality. This is not easy to achieve, although the Royal Embroiderers' Guild at Prince's Gate in London have a certain selection. If the materials are of poor quality the finished article will look cheap and wear badly. It is also important that the sequins should be small — large gold plastic ones simply do not look nice and, as in the case of poor gold thread, the colour wears off or tarnishes. Since any hand embroidery involves a lot of work, it is better to do without the gold rather than use materials which will ruin rather than enhance the effect.

At roughly the same level of difficulty are the embroideries of Rabat and Tétouan. In the case of Rabat embroidery, the problem is one of design and choice of colours, rather than stitches. Tétouan work at its best (the Fitzwilliam Museum *tensifa*, for example) is undoubtedly taxing, on the level of the finest pieces from Algiers, but for the less ambitious there are all kinds of possibilities.

The individual elements from Tétouan embroidery can, for example, very easily be taken and copied — in the corner of a scarf, or in a band on the edge of a hand-towel or tray-cloth. As long as the traditional colour combinations are respected and the paler shades outlined with a thin dark line of back-stitch, the effect can hardly fail to be cheerful and pleasant. Long and short stitch, or any stitch which gives this sort of effect ≡≡≡≡ can be used perfectly well. A single floral group or "cone" can even be blown up and worked in wool to make a cushion cover. In this case, it is advisable to chose a white or neutral ground in the 18th-century manner, since the thickness and relative lack of lustre of the wool, together with the greater size of the motif, can look rather coarse and heavy against a coloured material.

Those fairly confident of their colour sense could certainly get very good and original effects by taking isolated Rabat motifs and embroidering them in the centre of a cushion, to decorate a towel, or, very large, in the middle of a bedspread, with one of the border designs to make an edge. Wool obviously does not have the sheen of silk, but if one of the glossier types, available at least in Europe, were chosen, the effect would be particularly good. The question of colour is less easily solved. Ideally, it is preferable to go and look at a fair number of pieces to get an idea of the Rabat taste, but this is difficult outside Paris and, of course, Morocco. A very rough guide

Raf-Raf — flower from a mwasma tunic.

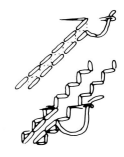

Diagonal Chevron Stitch Variants of this and of Single Fagotting are much used, especially in the embroidery of Fez.

Stem Stitch This is a very basic stitch in North African embroidery and one much used as a filling. ma'alka

Tétouan motif

Turkish – Spray of flowers stylised into squares and the "squares" arranged in rows

Algerian Star Stitch Tight stitches radiating out from the point in the cloth. The needle always passes through exactly in the same place, so that when the star is completed there is a hole in the centre. Zeliledj

would be to use the kind of colours and gradations traditional for Florentine *punta fiamma*.

P. Ricard in his admirable and exhaustive book draws, more or less life-size, a complete range of Rabat patterns which would be perfect to copy; it is available to Londoners in the library of the Victoria and Albert Museum.

Turkish embroidery is, to my mind, one of the most charming of all Islamic embroidery styles. The finest pieces are, of course, extremely difficult to reproduce – they are really at a professional level – but nevertheless the simpler ones can also be very attractive. Once the stitches have been mastered, the best plan is to copy one of the bunches of flowers (the Victoria and Albert Museum have a good teaching collection available), ideally on to the kind of cotton or linen with a very clear weave that the Turks themselves favoured.

In fact, anyone with a real interest in drawing inspiration from Oriental embroideries would do well to consider Turkish work seriously. The delicate colours, the flowers, the individuality of the pieces, make it particularly attractive and although a certain technical competence is required, the stitches are few and not hard to learn. After all, it should be remembered that the skill required is less than that of – say – the Victorian white worker; in other words that which tens of thousands of women possessed less than a century ago.

It would certainly be amusing to see a tablecloth embroidered with typically English flowers, such as sweetpeas, violets or lilies of the valley, done in the Turkish manner, or a scarf with ends worked with half-timbered cottages flanked by flowering fruit trees, instead of the usual kiosks and cypresses along the Bosphorus. In Turkish embroidery the colours are most important. Garishness spoils most of the pieces produced this century. For some reason (and aniline dyes are surely not the whole story) it is *very* difficult, once the tradition has been broken, to evolve colour schemes that are cheerful and not loud. For the technical aspects of Turkish embroidery, I warmly recommend Mrs Ramazanoğlu's work (see bibliography).

The two most difficult types of embroidery are, perhaps, the lovely purple pieces from Algeria and the gold work. The former because of its fineness, the latter because of the specialised techniques involved. Really, both require some level of professional training; but, of course, if anyone should attempt a piece of Algerian purple work, how lovely! And, in the hope that they do, I have put in the diagrams of the necessary stitches.

Although the sequin gold work is probably not something many would want to imitate except perhaps for Church vestments and banners, the motifs are interesting and well worth collecting and copying in other types of embroidery.

The couched gold work on the Moknine tunics involves a very special technique and again could not be recommended to the inexperienced. The tunics do, however, offer various design ideas — that of embroidering motifs from stone reliefs or even metal work in registers could be adapted to all sorts of other stitches to make long panels down the centre of a curtain, for example, or on a bedspread.

*Satin Stitch
This, with Long and Short Stitch, is again basic, especially at Rabat. Menezzel*

Again, although this type of gold couching — and indeed gold work in general — is difficult, attractive effects can be obtained by couching coloured cord on to a firm plain-coloured background, first lightly drawing free-hand an outline for the cord to cover. This is a well-known technique in North Africa, especially for men's clothes, where the cord or braid is the same colour as the background material. It is not difficult to get the knack of it in its simpler forms and as it is quite quick, it can be used to cover comparatively large surfaces. It should be remembered, however, that it is not suitable in places which get a lot of wear, such as chair seats.

Another possibility, although not strictly embroidery, which these tunics and those of Nabeul suggest, is the use of appliqué ribbons — a particularly pretty and again simple and quick way of edging curtains, lengthening a child's dress, decorating cushions, or adding interest to a plain straight dress.

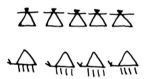

Nabeul — row of brides in the position of jelwa and row of camels carrying brides in litters from the "sample" panel of a Nabeul tunic, worked in pastel satin stitch

Lastly, I would like to set down five points which I have occasionally found helpful and encouraging in the course of a number of years handling — and even doing — embroidery.

(1)   Anyone who can thread a needle can produce a piece of needlework — and I am of course including all who use needle-threaders!

(2)   Particularly for a first attempt, chose something suited to your skill, capacity for perserverance (only you can judge this) and the time available. It is much more satisfactory to have an embroidered apron which took two days to complete and will be useful for years, than the miserable consciousness of drawers full of unfinished over-ambitious projects. Unfinished projects can be expensive too.

(3)   Do not be depressed at not being able to achieve the finest work. All countries have "rustic" versions of their "court" styles and, as long as they are reasonably tidily done, they can well have more charm than the official-looking productions. Indeed, the perfection of certain professional pieces may be such that they look machine-made, which defeats the whole purpose.

Double darning — meterrha.

(4)   Over colours, be cautious – I don't mean dismal, but North African embroideries will not come out well in the shades of brown, arsenic green and day-glo orange you happen to find at the bottom of your aunt's work-basket. Over patterns, less rather than more is a golden rule.

(5)   *Whatever* you produce will be more interesting than a mass-produced kit. It will show your taste, personality, imagination – and courage. After all, the North African women who made the embroideries in this book were born to it. You will be doing something completely original and new. So, I very much hope that you will have as much fun working embroideries as I did writing about them. Good luck!

Caroline Stone
May 4th, 1984
Via di Grotta Pinta 10 int 8
Rome
Italy

*"We protected you in this world
Protect us in the next."*

Saying from El Djem, on cutting a length of cloth from the loom or finishing a piece of work.

Gilt appliqué Chéchaouen star.

Acknowledgements

All the embroideries in this book are the property of the author, except for the following:

The Whitworth Art Gallery, the University of Manchester depicted on pages 18, 21, 33, 45, 66.

The Fitzwilliam Museum, Cambridge on pages 73, 94.

Esther Fitzgerald Textiles, London on pages 69, 90.

to all of whom the warmest gratitude is extended for their help

Map by Swanston Graphics, Derby, England

GLOSSARY

'ain Eye; here particularly the evil eye

'ajar Wall hanging, generally hung horizontally

'aleuj Convert to Islam; renegado; a style of embroidery

alkantir (al-kantir) Tubular metal beads

'amud Pillars; tall embroidery motif from El Djem

'aqrab Crab or scorpion; embroidery motif

'arid Decorative strips hung on walls or above bed niches

'attabi Tabby cloth – watered silk

'attar Scent

bahnug Tie-dyed head-coverings from the Berber region of Chenini

bait House; section or repeat of an embroidery pattern

baraka Blessing

barmaqli A Turkish open-work stitch often done with flat metal thread.
The folk etymology derives it from the famous Barmakid family,
although in fact it comes from the Turkish word for fretted
wooden screens, which the stitch resembles

beskri Elaborately patterned woven silk from Djerba

besmaq Wooden shoes; an embroidery pattern

bint duka Daughter of the *duka*, smaller version of the Sousse
headdress – see *duka*

bniqa (also *benika*) Hair covering, particularly for use at the baths
(Tétouan and Algiers) (see Ingres)

buraq Mythical steed which bore the Prophet on his Night Journey

burnous Hooded, sleeved over-robe worn by men

camisa margomada Andalusian ancestor of Raf-Raf tunics

cartonna Marriage tunics of Kaala Kbira, so-called from the layers of
card used to stiffen them

chadur Veil worn by the women of Iran

chandora Veil of Shingiti and Walata women south of the Sahara; from
Chandor on the west coast of India

chebka Pillow lace (Tunis) and in particular inserts of lace

chechia (sheshiya) A fez

dallala "Guide" or go-between

derra Scarf worn on the shoulders (Fez)

dohla Gold-embroidered marriage tunic of Hammamet

driboz Pillow lace (Algeria)

duka Headdress of Sousse

farmla Sleeveless jacket, principally worn by women and boys

farmla bej-jawanah Jacket with wings, so-called on account of its
enormous stiffened epaulets

al-fatiha   The first seven verses of the Koran

fatwa   A formal legal opinion

fraja   A caftan-shaped over-garment, traditionally worn over caftan and *juha*

funduk   A warehouse, especially for foreign merchants and, by extension, inn or caravansarai

furoshiki   (Japan) Square piece of material originally used for sitting on in the bath, now used as a carrying cloth

futa   The veil of Gabès

gad Zazia   A geometric motif, named after Zazia (Djaziya), the heroine of the folk epic of the Beni Hilal (south Tunisia)

gamra/qamra   Full moon motif, common in Tunisian embroideries

gelsa   Embroidered square napkin used to mark the places of the guests of honour (Fez)

geniza   A room in a synagogue used as a depository for written documents which might bear the name of God and hence cannot be destroyed

glastra   Vase of flowers – name for that embroidery pattern at Rhodes

gonbaiz   Richly embroidered jacket with splendid buttons, part of Moroccan Jewish marriage costume (see Delacroix)

gourgaf/gorgaf   Low rectangular embroidery frame of Turkish origin

guza   Walnut; hence oval embroidery motif

hadith   A story or saying attributed to the Prophet or one of his companions and collected in the early days of Islam from those who knew them personally. This body of tradition is one of the major sources of Islamic Law, the other being the Koran

haik   Length of cloth; cloth worn by men, especially Berbers, instead of a cloak; women's veil

hajjiya   A woman who has made the pilgrimage (*hajj*) to Mecca

halwa   Sweets

hammam   Turkish bath

hellal   The large silver fibulae used to hold up the *hellala* (q.v.)

hellala   The length of cloth worn by women in many rural areas of Tunisia, held by one or two fibulae and a belt

hezam   Wide velvet belt heavily embroidered in gold, particularly that of the Moroccan Jewish women

hilal   Crescent moon

hit susi (*khit susi*)   Strong linen thread used in gold embroidery, the best being from Sousse in Tunisia

hiti (*haiti/hayti*; plural *hiyati*)   Wall-hangings for houses or tents and, sometimes, mosques

hram   Draped dress of El Djem

huli   Draped dress of Nefta and Tozeur

hut ala ras-ak   A fish on your head; expression of good augury (Tunisia)

izar (plural: *izur*)   Great embroidered curtains, especially from Rabat

jebba   A long-sleeved, chemise-type robe; sometimes used more generally for other types of dress or tunic

jebba el-ain fil-ain Another name for *dohla* (q.v.); literally, the tunic of the eye against the eye

jebba matruza Parti-coloured dress of Hammamet

jehfa camel-litter

jellaba Robe

jelteta Wrap-over skirt heavily embroidered in gold, part of Moroccan Jewish marriage costume

jelwa Ceremony of the presentation of the bride

jerid Display of horsemanship; fantasia

jihad Holy war

juha (jukha) A caftan-shaped tunic in broadcloth, sometimes bottom-most of a set of three robes

kadrun Black wool-gauze robe from Hammamet

kebba Handsome woollen burnous worn by notables on ceremonial occasions (Tunisia)

kettafiya Small rectangular cloth spread on the shoulders during hairdressing (Tétouan and Tozeur)

khetem Sidna Sliman The seal of our Lord Solomon; a hexagonal lace pattern

khinjar Dagger

khomsa/khumsa Having five; the sign of the hand with fingers spread, one of the most auspicious symbols throughout North Africa and elsewhere in the Middle East

kissaria Market-place

kiswa Dress; embroidered covering of saint's tomb; the large gold-embroidered covering of the *ka'aba* at Mecca

el-kiswa el-kebira Golden marriage tunic of Hammamet (see also *dohla* and *jebba el-ain fil-ain*)

kiswa al-kabira As above, means the great tunic; bridal dress, especially of Moroccan Jews

kubba (qubba) Cupola; hence "saint's" tomb

libas Clothing

lingache (lingas) Bobbin lace (Rabat); perhaps from *lingas* – pear, after the shape of the bobbins

ma'allema Woman teacher; in this book always used for a teacher of embroidery

majlis Reception room

makhzen Central government and, by extension, the Royal Cities of Morocco

malf Woollen cloth, originally from Amalfi

malti Very ordinary cotton cloth, perhaps originally from Malta

marabout Holy man

mashallah What God wills – pious phrase common in calligraphic embroidery

mashrabiya Fretted wooden screens

massar shiar Literally, "hair squeezer"; Aleppan word for cloth used to tie up hair in the bath

melhafa Geometrically woven silk veil, apparently made by the Jewish women of the Gabès region for a Muslim clientèle; it was the word for veil in Muslim Andalusia

mellah Jewish quarter

mendil Square piece of cloth

mendil el-mjamar Literally, brazier cloth; embroidered cloth used for wrapping packets of clothes; the name may come from the stylized floral motifs or, possibly, from the custom of perfuming garments with the smoke of scented woods

mendila Little girls' tie-dyed shawls from Chenini

menorah A seven-branched candelabra used by the Jews

merbet (plural: *mrabet*) Pleated gaiters reaching from knee to ankle (Fez) worn by women

mesloul (*meslul*) Band of drawn-thread work or needle-weaving

mhedda (plural: *mhadd*) Large rectangular or long thin bolster-shaped cushion

mherma Handkerchief

mjadli General word for braids, trimmings, etc

mlaya Veil worn by black women of Algeria

mressa Vase for sprinkling rose-water, hence tear-drop embroidery motif

mwasma Literally tattooed; used for the third-day marriage tunic of Raf-Raf

neggafa Mistress of ceremonies (Fez)

nhar tangiz ala al-hut Day of Jumping over the Fish; part of the wedding ceremony at Sfax

pnit A loop of bobbin lace; the initial p suggests that it is Judaeo-Arabic

qaba Close-fitting wide-sleeved robe from 10th-century Baghdad

qadi One who administers Islamic law

qamis Chemise or tunic

qmejja A simple rectangular tunic worn under formal costumes (Hammamet); a gold couched tunic (Moknine)

qufiya (sometimes transliterated *keffiya*) Coif or headdress

randa Pillow lace (Rabat)

raqama To embroider

ras al-arusa Head of the bride; a Salé embroidery pattern

rassama Woman who drew the design (*rasm*) on cloth for the embroideress, but did not necessarily work it (Hammamet)

rechem (*resem/resm*) The outline drawn on the cloth for the embroideress to work (Tétouan)

ribat Fortress for men dedicated to holy war

sanaa A trained embroideress, but not necessarily a teacher

sarma High, metal, conical headdress over which a veil was draped, worn by married women in Algeria *sarwal*   Trousers

sau   Rectangular cloth with heavy borders used for tying up the hair in the bath (Meknès)

sefseri   Tunisian veil

setteba   Broom – an embroidery pattern

shahadah   Muslim profession of faith

shamsa   A motif half-way between a sun and a flower, said to symbolize the light of religion; common on scholars' robes, often embroidered over the heart

sharif (feminine *sharifa*)   One claiming descent from the Prophet's family

sirwal bid-duka   Trousers with triangular embroidery panels, echoing the conical shape of the *duka* (q.v.) headdress (Tunis)

sparver   Bed-tent from the Greek Islands

sraref   Crenellations – an embroidery pattern

souriya (*suriya*)   Hand-woven linen, perhaps originally from Syria (Tunisia)

surah   Chapter of the Koran

suriya mabdu   Everyday tunic from Raf-Raf

swiqat   Embroidered leggings from Bizerte

tahlil   Couched and braided work, particularly used for decorating necks and fronts of men's robes; now sometimes applied to the chain-stitch used as a cheap modern substitute

tahzim   Putting on the belt, a ceremony which takes place after the consummation of the marriage (Tunisia)

tal   Flat metal thread

tala   Minaret-shaped embroidery up the seam of Rabat hangings

tanbit   Couching

tanquila (*tanqila*)   Sampler (Hammamet)

tantoura (*tantura*)   High conical headdress of the Druze women of Lebanon

taqrita m'asfra   Little bird scarf – headdress from Raf-Raf

tarf el-ktef   Red woollen shoulder shawl worn draped around the body and pinned at the shoulder (Kerkenna)

tarf er-ras   Red woollen head shawl of Kerkenna

teffaha   Apple; circular embroidery motif

telleqa   Sampler (Morocco)

tensifa   Very long narrow mirror cover (Tétouan)

tesrif   Pillow lace (Tunis)

tiraz   Official factories which produced cloth or clothing for the ruler, with woven or embroidered calligraphic inscriptions; the cloth itself. Secondarily, embroidery – see *triz, triza, terz*

telmita (plural: *tlamet*)   Mattress cover (Fez)

terz d-el-ghorza   Embroidery from Fez – counted thread work

terz meknassi   Embroidery from Meknès

terz d-es-sqalli   Gold embroidery, generally held to be "embroidery of

Sicily"

tkek Draw-string or sash for baggy trousers

tlamt d-el khrib Bed valance (Fez)

tobaza Small hanging used as wedding decoration by the Jews of Rabat

triz et-telli Coloured wool embroidery on net especially from Raf-Raf

triza kahla Solid black embroidery (Tunisian coastal region)

tughra Formal signature of the Ottoman Sultans

yashmak Turkish form of face veil

yukata (Japanese) Japanese cotton kimono for informal wear

zaouia (*zawiya*) The establishment of a religious order, in some ways comparable to a monastery

zellij Tile; hence a number of square and rectangular embroidery motifs

As Arabic plurals are complicated and confusing, plurals have been made in a rather illiterate way by adding s to the singular: one *tensifa,* two *tensifas*

Sources of quotations not credited fully in the text

For aesthetic reasons some quotations used have not been fully credited in the text. The following list is a guide to those instances.

pp 7, 30, 90, 172, 182   LUNDE, Paul and WINTLE, Justin   *A Dictionary of Islamic Proverbs*   Routledge & Kegan Paul

p7   STONE, Caroline   *The Traditions of the Women drawn from Bukhari*   unpublished

p 12   MASUDI   *The Meadows of Gold* vol IV, translated by Paul Lunde and Caroline Stone   Routledge & Kegan Paul 1985

pp 28, 58   MARÇAIS, W.   *Textes arabes de Tanger*   Paris 1911

pp 30, 96   OUGOUAG-KEZZAL, C.   "Quelques aspects de la vie feminine à Tlemcen"   *Libyca*, vol XXV, 1977, pp 299-317

pp 35, 37, 50, 76, 79   JOUIN, Jeanne   "Chansons de l'Escarpolette à Fès et Rabat-Salé"   *Hésperis* 1954, pp 341-63

pp 38, 43, 74   JOUIN, Jeanne   "Chansons d'Amour"   *Hesperis* 1954 (304), pp 1-23

p 47   JUSTINARD, L.   "Notes d'historie et de litterature Berbère"   *Hesperis* V 1925, pp 227-38 (collected from the Chleuh of Sous in Morocco)

p 87   Anon. poem from Muslim Spain translated by Paul Lunde

p 90   OUGOUAG-KEZZAL, C.   "Bref apercu Historique sur la broderie arabe, sur une vieille broduese au coeur d'Alger"   *Libyca*, vol XVII, 1969, pp 343-8

p107   MARTY, Paul   "Chants Lyriques Populaires du Sud Tunisien"   *Revue Tunisienne*, 1936 (1) pp 111-35

p 111   *The Romance of the People of the Crescent Moon*, translated by Paul Lunde and Caroline Stone   unpublished

pp 112, 121, 123, 202   COMBES, J. & S. and LOUIS, A.   "Autour du travail de la laine (Djerba)"   *IBLA* IX, 1946, pp 51-75

p 119   ZOUARI, Ali   "Sana et maalma dans le région de Sfax"   *CATP* vol II, 1968, pp 29-32

pp 128, 166   MARTY, Paul   "Chants Lyriques Populaires du Sud Tunisien"   *Revue Tunisienne*, 1936 (2) pp 256-95

p 138   MASUDI   *The Meadows of Gold and Mines of Precious Stones* vol I, translated by Paul Lunde and Caroline Stone   Routledge & Kegan Paul 1984

p 151   SUGIER, Clémence   "Le thème du lion dans les arts populaires tunisiens"   *CATP* vol III, 1969, pp 67-84

p 157   Folk song variants current in North Africa for four centuries

p 174   Current saying, Tunis

BIBLIOGRAPHY

The following abbreviations have been used in the bibliography:

Afr. FR   *Afrique Français*
B.M.M.A.   *Bulletin of the Metropolitan Museum of Art*
C.A.T.P.   *Cahiers des arts et traditions populaires*
C.T.   *Cahiers de Tunisie*
H.T.   *Hespéris Tamuda*
J.R.A.S.   *Journal of the Royal Asiatic Society*
R.E.I.   *Revue des Etudes Islamiques*
Rev.Afr.   *Revue Africaine*
R.T.   *Revue Tunisienne*

ALGERIA

BEL, Marguerite A. *Les Arts Indigènes Féminins en Algérie*, Alger 1939

Catalogue of Algerian Embroideries, Victoria and Albert Museum, London 1935

MARÇAIS, Georges "Les Broderies Turques d'Alger", *Ars Islamica*, IV, 1937, pp 146-7

MARÇAIS, Georges *Le Musée Stephane Gsell: Musée des Antiquités et d'Art Musulman d'Alger*, Alger 1950

OUGOUAG-KEZZAL, C. "Bref aperçu historique sur la broderie arabe, sur un vieille brodeuse au coeur d'Alger" *Libyca*, vol XVII, 1969, pp 343-348

Costumes and Customs

ADAM, A. "Le costume dans quelques tribus de l'Anti-Atlas", *H.T.* vol 39, 1952, pp 459-485

BEN TANFOUS, Aziza "Les ceintures de femmes en Tunisie", *C.A.T.P.* vol IV, 1971, pp 103-122

BOURGEOT, A. "Le Costume Masculin des Kel Ahaggar" *Libyca*, vol XVII, 1969, pp 355-376

ESQUER, G. "Le costume algérois d'après un ouvrage récent", *Rev. Afr.*, vol 72, 1931, pp 91-101

GAUDRY, M. "Une exposition de travaux d'arts féminins indigènes", *Afr. Fr.*, vol 43, 1933, pp 461-466

JOUIN, Jeanne *Chansons de l'Escarpolette à Fès et Rabat-Salé*, Hespéris, 1954, pp 341-363

JOUIN, Jeanne "Iconographie de la mariée citadine dans l'Islam

Nord-Africain", *R.E.I.*, vol 5, 1931, pp 313-339

LEVY, R. "Notes on Costumes from Arabic Sources" *J.R.A.S.,* 1935, pp 318-338

MAHJOUB, Naziha "La circoncision dans une famille bourgeoise traditionelle de Tunis autour des années 30" *C.A.T.P.* vol VI, 1976, pp 121-134

MAHJOUB, Naziha "Le costume hanéfite des hommes de religion et de justice à Tunis" *C.A.T.P.* vol II, 1968, pp 79-92

MARÇAIS, Georges *Le Costume Musulman d'Alger*, Paris, 1930

MASMOUDI, M. ed. – (various authors) *Les Costumes Traditionnels Féminins de Tunisie* Maison Tunisienne de l'Edition Tunis, 1978

MOHAMMAD, Lakdar Si. *Rites de mariage chez les Beni Mtir et Ait Ayyache* Congrès des Sociétés Savantes de l'Afrique du Nord II 1938, p 785

OUGOUAG-KEZZAL-C. "Le Costume et la Parure de la Mariée à Tlemcen" *Libyca*, vol XVIII, 1970, pp 253-267

PUIGAUDEAU, Odette du "Arts et coutumes des Maures III" *H.T.* vol XI, 1970, pp 5-82

RUBENS, Alfred *A History of Jewish Costume* Weidenfeld and Nicolson, London 1967 and 1973

SETHOM, Samira "La confection du costume féminin d'Hammamet", *C.A.T.P.* vol I, 1968, pp 105-111

SETHOM, Samira "Relations inter-régionales et costumes féminins dans la presqu'île du Cap Bon" *C.A.T.P.* vol VI, 1976, pp. 101-108

SETHOM, Samira et al. *Signes et Symboles dans l'Art Populaire Tunisien* S.T.D., Publishers, Tunis, 1976

SETHOM, Samira "La Tunique de Mariage en Tunisie", *C.A.T.P.* vol III, 1969, pp 5-20

SKHIRI, Fathia "Les Châles des Matmata", *C.A.T.P.* vol IV, 1971, pp 49-53

SUGIER, Clémence "Les coiffes féminines de Tunisie", *C.A.T.P.* vol II, 1968, pp 61-78

ZOUARI, Ali "Le Mariage Traditionnel à Sfax (Arabic article with French summary)" *C.A.T.P.* vol VII, 1980, pp 157-8

Mediterranean

BERNIS, Carmen, *Indumentaria Medieval Española*, Instituto Diego Velazquez del Consejo Superior de las investigaciones cientificas, Madrid 1956

JOHNSTONE, Pauline, *Byzantine Tradition in Church Embroidery,* London 1967

JOHNSTONE, Pauline, *Greek Island Embroidery* Alec Tiranti, London 1961

LOMBARD, Maurice, *Les textiles dans le mond musulman VIIe-XIIe siècle*, Paris 1978

SERGEANT, R.B., *Islamic Textiles*, Librairie du Liban, Beirut 1972

STAPLEY, Mildred, *Popular Weaving and Embroidery in Spain*, London, 1920s

WEIR, Shelagh, *Palestinian Embroidery*, British Museum, London 1970

Morocco

ALAOUI, Fatima, *Manuel de Broderie Marocaine Classique*, Salé 1969

BEY RIOTTOT, Olagnier, *Influence Turque dans la broderie de Tétouan au Maroc*, Ist Int. Cong. of Turkish Arts, Ankara 1959 (communications 1961) pp 291-96

BRUNOT-DAVID, C., *Les Broderies de Rabat*, Collection Hespéris IX, Rabat 1943

DIMAND, M.S., "An Exhibition of North African Textiles", *B.M.M.A.* (N.S.) I 1942-3 p 4

"The Embroideries of Morocco", *B.M.M.A.* 19 1924 pp 32-34

GAYOT, H. and MINAULT, Mme, *La broderie de Salé moderne*, Ecole du Livre, Rabat 1955

GOICHON, A.M. "La broderie au fil d'or á Fès" *Hespéris* vol XXVI 1939 pp 49-85 and 241-281

GUÉRARD, Martha "Contribution à l'art de la broderie au Maroc I (Fès)" *H.T.* vol VIII 1967 pp 5-22

GUÉRARD, Martha, "Contribution à l'étude de l'art de la broderie au Maroc II (Fès – 'Aleuj – et Rabat)", *H.T.* vol IX 1968 pp 123-156

GUÉRARD, Martha, "Contribution à l'étude de l'art de la broderie au Maroc III (Tétouan et Alger)", *H.T.* vol X fasc.I 1969 pp 191-216

GUÉRARD, Martha, "Contribution à l'étude de l'art de la broderie au Maroc IV (Chéchaouen)", *H.T.* vol XV 1974 pp 225-250

GUÉRARD, Martha, "Contribution à l'étude de l'art de la broderie au Maroc V (Salé)", *HT* vol XVIII 1978-9 pp 211-232

JOUIN, Jeanne, "Les Thèmes Décoratifs des Broderies Marocains", *Hespéris* vol 15 1932 pp 11-30, vol 25 1935 pp 149-166

LARREA, A. de *El bordado en Sidi Ifni*, Archivos del Instituto de Estudios Africanos vol 7 no.31 1954 pp 15-29

NAVICET, L.J. Mme, "Le filet brodé marocain", *France-Maroc* no.15 mai 1917

RICARD, P., *Arts Marocains I Broderies*, Alger 1918

RICARD, PROSPER and KOUADRI, MOHAMMED, *Procédés Marocains de Teinture des Laines – Les Préceptes du Vieux Teinturier*, Ecole du Livre, Rabat, 1938

ROSS, D.W., "Some Textiles from Morocco", *Bulletin of the Museum of Fine Arts*, Boston, vol 20, 1922, pp 36-39

TOWNSHEND, G., "Moroccan and Algerian Textiles", Bulletin of the Museum of Fine Arts, Boston, vol 26, 1928, p 110

Tunisia

BAUDIN, Y. and OSSIPOV, M. *Broderie de Kerkenna sur toile, Etude d'éléments*, Office des Arts Tunisiens, Centre de Sfax, 1955

COMBÈS, J. and S., "Autour du travail de la laine (Djerba)," *I.B.L.A.* vol 33, part I, 1946, pp 51-75

GINESTOUS, L. Mme. "La tunique brodée de Rafraf", *Bulletin de liaison de l'Office des Arts Tunisiens* vol I, 1954, pp 13-20

GINESTOUS, P. "Bizerte et sa région – la vie artisanale", *I.B.L.A.* vol XIX, 1956, pp 93-114

GOLVIN, L. and LOUIS, A., "Les Tisseuses de la Région Sfaxienne", *I.B.L.A.* vol 12, 1949, pp 237-262

JOUIN, J., "Le taref des Kerkeniennes", *Revue d'Études Islamiques* 1948, pp 51-53

LOUIS, André, "Sellerie d'apparat et selliers à Tunis", *C.A.T.P.* vol I, 1968, pp 41-100

REVAULT, J., "Broderies Tunisiennes", *Cahiers de Tunisie* vol 8, 1960, pp 137-157

SPEZZAFUMO DE FAUCEMBERGE, S., *Dentelles et broderies tunisiennes*, Deplanche, Paris 1931

SUGIER, Clémence "Le thème du lion dans les arts populaires tunisiens" *C.A.T.P.* vol III, 1969, pp 67-84

   Traité pratique de la dentelle Arabe chebka, Les Soeurs Blanches de Notre Dame d'Afrique de la Marsa Collection Cartier Bresson, early 20th century

ZOUARI, Ali "Sanaa et maalma dans la région de Sfax" *C.A.T.P.* vol II, 1968, pp 29-32

Turkish embroidery

BLACK, David and LOVELESS, Clive *Işlemeler, Ottoman Domestic Embroideries* London, 1978

BEN TANFOUS, Aziza, "al-Tatriz al-Turki", *C.A.T.P.* vol VII, 1980 pp 25-32

BERKER, Nurhayat, "Islemeler" Yapi ve Kredi Bankasi, Istanbul, 1981

BERRY, Burton Yost, "Old Turkish Towels I", *Art Bulletin* vol XIV no.4 Dec 1932 pp 344-358
   "Old Turkish Towels II", *Art Bulletin* (N.S.) vol II no.3 Sept 1938 pp 251-265

ÇORUM, Bengi, "Turkish Embroidery" *Akbank'in Bir Kültür Hizmeti* Hizmeti, Istanbul, 20th century

GENTLES, Margaret, *Turkish and Greek Island Embroideries* The Art Institute of Chicago, 1964

GÖNÜL, Macide, "Turk Elioleri Sant I, XVI-XIX yüzyil", Turkiye is Bankasi Kültür Yayinlani

MARÇAIS, Georges, "Les Broderies Turques d'Alger", *Ars Islamica* vol IV 1937 pp 146-7

RAMAZANOĞLU, Gülseren, *Turkish Embroidery,* Van Nostrand

Reinhold, New York 1976

TACISER, Onuk, *Igñe Oyalari – Needleworks*, Turkiye Bankasi, Istanbul 1981

Turkish Folk Embroideries, Museum of Mankind, London 1981

Turk Islemelerinden Ornekler, Akbank, Istanbul 1970s

Stitches

CHRISTIE, Archibald Mrs, *Samplers and Stitches*, Batsford, London 1920

DILLMONT, Th. de, *Encyclopédie des ouvrages des dames*, Paris

SCHÉFER, G. and AMIS, S., *Travaux manuels et Economie domestique*, Paris

THOMAS, Mary *Dictionary of Stitches*, Hodder and Stoughton, London 1981

INDEX